God's Bucket List

God's Bucket List

Heaven's Surefire Way to Happiness

in This Life and Beyond

TERESA TOMEO

IMAGE
New York

Copyright © 2013 by Teresa Tomeo Communications, LLC

All rights reserved.
Published in the United States by Image,
an imprint of the Crown Publishing Group,
a division of Random House LLC, a Penguin
Random House Company, New York.
www.crownpublishing.com

IMAGE is a registered trademark, and the "I" colophon
is a trademark of Random House LLC.

Library of Congress Cataloging-in-Publication Data
is available upon request.

ISBN 978-0-385-34690-0
eISBN 978-0-385-34691-7

PRINTED IN THE UNITED STATES OF AMERICA

Jacket design by Jessie Sayward Bright
Jacket art: bobvidler/Getty Images, borisz/Getty Images

10 9 8 7 6 5 4 3 2 1

First Edition

Contents

A New Twist on the Bucket List

 *But seek first His Kingdom and His righteousness
and all these things will be given to you as well.*
—Matthew 6:33

Do you have a bucket list, an itinerary of things you
want to do before you die? Maybe you want to swim
with dolphins or live in Italy for a year. Maybe you
want to hike as far as you can toward the summit of
Mount Everest or ride the teacups at Disney World
for the very first time. Maybe you want to parachute
out of an airplane or explore an underwater ship-
wreck off the coast of Florida. Or maybe you just
want to spend a month at the beach and read all the
books you've been meaning to for the last number of
years. At the heart of all of these dreams is the desire
for adventure, for new experiences. Now, what if we
suppose that besides all these things that you want
to do in your life before you pass on to the next, God
has a bucket list for you, an agenda of adventures He
wants you to experience, ways of living before you
die? Okay, granted, this list doesn't exist (unless you

want to consider God's commandments a bucket list). I'm not suggesting I've found some secret scroll that requires that we all dance at a luau, but what if God does have a list of things we should do before we die?

This book is about that *what if* question. This book is also about, well, me and my struggles to figure out what God might want for me before I kick the proverbial bucket. I tell the stories that follow in the hopes that there may be something in my life that mirrors your own and that I can be a helpful hand during uncertain times or a warm smile when you feel like life might be getting the best of you. In any event, I like to tell stories, and—in order to explore this imagined idea of a heavenly list of ways to live and things to do—that's what I'm going to do. So let's begin with one.

"You're so lucky," I overheard one woman say to another while I was shopping at my local Italian market one afternoon. "That's definitely on my bucket list."

Now, by "overheard" I really mean eavesdropping. I admit it, I sometimes *accidently* overhear things that others are talking about, but that's just because I'm so interested in people. Really!

I started to move a little closer, trying to listen as intently as possible to what it was that was on this woman's bucket list. But I bumped into some tomatoes in the produce aisle, sending them everywhere and blowing my cover. When I looked up, the two women had moved on.

Despite my lousy attempt at playing James Bond I was able to catch enough of their conversation to realize they were talking about a wished-for something. Maybe it was a vacation, or a journey to see the pyramids, or bungee jumping. But for me, this exchange represented a sort of confirmation. Almost everyone has a bucket list—a list of things to do before "kicking the bucket." Even me.

I have to admit I'd never heard of a bucket list before the film *The Bucket List*. Jack Nicholson and Morgan Freeman play two terminally ill older men from very different backgrounds who become unlikely friends while undergoing chemotherapy together. When each is given less than a year to live, they decide to make the most of the time they have left. After each makes up a bucket list of places to go, things to do, and people to reconcile with, they set off on a combined journey to fulfill their lists—with sometimes funny, sometimes sad results.

That movie made me think about my own "life list." I love lists, and even though I didn't call it a bucket list, for most of my life I'd had a list of things that I wanted to accomplish in my life. In my twenties and thirties I worked feverishly to cross off this and that, and in my eyes I was quite successful. My goal after graduating from journalism school was to make a name for myself in the broadcast news business, preferably in my hometown of Detroit, which was among the top-ten TV and radio markets in the country. It didn't matter that the standard operating procedure for starry-eyed broadcast news newbies was to pack up and head for Podunk, Idaho, or some other obscure location to supposedly work their way up the media ladder. That was fine for some with lower expectations and for those who were convinced they needed to follow all the so-called procedures and rules to a T. But procedures and rules were meant to be broken, so I went ahead and broke them and managed to land my first radio-news gig at an AM/FM station in suburban Detroit. It wasn't exactly the biggest outlet on the block; as a matter of fact, it was barely a blip on the media radar screen. But it had just what an ambitious and budding journalist needed. It had a decent news department that would allow me to cover some important stories and to rub elbows with the bigwigs.

My aggressive goal setting continued as I moved from one news department to the next, eventually landing my first big TV news gig by the time I was twenty-seven. For a while it was fun and exciting. In addition to pursuing and achieving my dreams, there were other benefits, including a certain amount of notoriety and a not-too-shabby paycheck. Along the way I was also blessed to meet and marry a great guy. This was one for the bonus category, as marriage was not an item on my bucket list.

In the end, though, in my mad desire to make a name for myself, I nearly lost everything that was important to me, personally and professionally. It was then that I realized that so many of our to-do lists, so many of our bucket lists, focus only on sensation and pleasure: swimming the Great Barrier Reef; climbing Mount Kilimanjaro (no way I, or most of us, could get up Everest); A, B, C. However, all these goals seemed to focus primarily on sensory experience. What about the spiritual things in life? Where was God in all of this?

He was, at least for me, nowhere to be found.

I am 100-percent Italian, with half of that Italian heritage coming from Calabria, a region in southern Italy whose residents are known for their extreme hardheadedness—the *testa dura* syndrome. In other words, sometimes we Calabrese types need a house to fall on us to get the message. I did indeed have a thrilling career racking up numerous awards for my coverage of everything from warehouse fires to plane crashes to downsizing in the automobile industry. However, while I loved covering breaking news in a

big city, in-depth reporting was much more rewarding, and I also earned recognition through several in-
vestigative series dealing with hard-hitting topics like
child abuse and local government corruption. Teresa
Tomeo became a household name in the Detroit news
market. My life was fast-paced and intense. My career
was all-consuming, leaving little room for anything
or anyone else. But at the time, and here comes the
testa dura syndrome again, I was enjoying the ride.
Little did I know or see that at the end of the ride was
a dead end.

Like many people, my career was at the top of my
bucket list. I wanted to become a successful journalist, and I worked hard to make that happen. I had an
exciting career, and before I knew it, almost twenty
years had gone by. And that's when I began having a
lot of second thoughts about my chosen profession. I
never imagined walking away from the news media.
I was, as I've already said, one of those lucky human
beings who knew from the time she was a child what
she wanted to do. And I can honestly say that up until
this crisis of faith in my career, I never had the desire
to do anything else. (Well, for a while there was the
dream of running away and trying out for the Radio
City Music Hall Rockettes.) I knew that I had to stick
with what I loved the most: the media.

Those doubts and second thoughts began to rain on

my parade thanks to some changes in the news business. All of a sudden, it was "so long" to serious news and "hello" to yet one more car crash, snowstorm, or murder. The thrill was gone. Sensationalism and ratings ruled the show. It was time to move on professionally, but move on to where, and to what? These questions were at the heart of my internal angst. At times I wanted to abandon the business, feeling disillusioned and worn out. Even so, this is what I had always wanted to do, and I could not possibly envision going through the day without being able to practice my craft. It just didn't seem right or fair to leave it.

At the time of this professional crisis, I had also become active in my Catholic faith again. Christians can be a great source of light and balance in secular newsrooms. But Christians are also supposed to be able to use their gifts the way God intended. How did chasing ambulances fit the call from our Lord in Scripture to be the salt of the earth and the light of the world? The thought did cross my mind that maybe I was reaping at least a bit of what I had sown during all those years of putting the job or the story first and everything else that should have mattered, especially my relationship with my husband—and, even more important, God—on the back burner.

Toward the end of my broadcast news career I had come to the realization, through a lot of trial and error, that achieving joy has nothing to do with destinations or dollar signs. God used the loss of my first high-profile TV news position to help me come to that sobering conclusion. There is nothing like standing on the unemployment line to catch your attention. The hours stretched into days, which stretched into six long months of not being on the air. I was never really told why I was let go, which is fairly common in the rough-and-tumble news business. Suddenly the sacrifice of so much time away from home, which once seemed so necessary to get ahead, really seemed foolish. Now all I had to show for my hard work was a severance check and eight weeks of unemployment benefits.

Thank goodness, God keeps His promises and never abandons us, despite our stubbornness and bad decisions. God began to reveal Himself to me through a husband who had found his own way back to the Catholic Church. I was blessed with a man who believed in me and in our marriage. He encouraged me to start to take my faith seriously. So I did, and we also began to work earnestly on rebuilding our relationship. When I finally did get back on the TV airwaves, I had my priorities straight and was once again eager to make a difference.

That's one of the reasons that finding myself at such another crossroad in my career was so challenging. If God was still driving this bus, it was time for me to really let go of the wheel. I might still be hard-headed, but at least the house didn't have to fall on me twice. Deep down, I knew that the real bucket list is already designed by none other than God Himself.

I had learned and was now being again reminded of how God's list is uniquely created with each of us individually in mind and yet applies to everyone in a universal way. It's not a lofty list that requires us to go around curing cancer, solving world hunger, or even solving the many issues in our own circle of family and friends (for some of us, myself included, this would be more difficult than negotiating peace in the Middle East). It's simply about putting our relationship with God first. When we do this, we will lead an abundant life. Don't believe me? Check out John, chapter 10:

> The thief comes only to steal and kill and destroy;
> I have come so that they may have life, and have it
> abundantly. (John 10:10)

The key to this grand way of living life is submitting to God's version of fulfillment and abundance instead of insisting He bless, approve, and put the final stamp on our version of things. And this is where I initially made my big bucket list mistake. I wanted a meaningful life on my terms. I thought submitting and seeking a life in God would be extremely limiting, totally unappealing, and would translate into becoming a cloistered nun, a missionary in Ethiopia, or something else contrary to what I thought I needed to be. I couldn't have been more wrong.

What is abundance? To have abundance means to possess "an extremely plentiful or oversufficient quantity or supply." Abundance is also described as "fullness." In other words, we are not talking about leftovers or the short end of the stick. We are talking about a type of real joy that is bigger, better, and much deeper than we may have imagined. That's because, quite frankly, God is a really big God. Just as the old Christian folk song proclaims, He really does "have the whole world is in His hands," and He wants to give it to us. The secret—and it's not really a secret at all, for it's written all over the Bible—is that His gift of abundance has to be on His terms, not ours. And when we can embrace this, we engage in God's bucket list.

But the question remains, How do we figure this all out? How do we come to find God's bucket list for our lives? We can start by embracing the belief that God is very large and very much in charge. That said, I read through the Bible a few times, looking for clues. Of course, neither the Old nor the New Testament uses the words "bucket list." We do have the Ten Commandments and the Sermon on the Mount—definite listings of things we should and shouldn't do. But over the last couple of years, I began asking myself what if there were an actual bucket list that God designed for us and wanted us to follow? What would be on it?

This book is a bit of a thought experiment (mixed with some personal stories to help keep me grounded, since sometimes my mind can really fly high, as well as go in sixteen different directions). I don't intend to play God here or to understand God. As the prophet Isaiah reminds us, good luck in trying to wrap your mind around the alpha and the omega, the beginning and the end:

> For my thoughts are not your thoughts, nor are your ways my ways. As high as the heavens are above the earth, so high are my ways above your ways and my thoughts above your thoughts. (Isaiah 55:8–9)

I may not be able to fully understand God, but through my own life's ups and downs I have come to know for certain that He loves us and wants to remain close to us. So it would stand to reason that His bucket list for us must be something pretty special. What I intend to do in this book is to imagine how God would apply His everlasting, unconditional love to a bucket list for you and for me. Maybe it includes a journey. Maybe it's all about building something or fulfilling a goal you were never quite able to achieve. While each bucket list is as unique as the person who makes it, God's bucket list provides a set of guiding principles to help all of us reach the ultimate goal: to better know God. And while I'm not a betting woman, if I were, I would bet that God's bucket list could help us lead fulfilled and love-driven lives. This is my intent for this book.

1.

Live with Stillness

 Be still and know that I am God
—Psalm 46:10

Ever have one of those days when you feel like that proverbial gerbil on the wheel? You're running like crazy and getting nowhere fast. Even after plowing through every item on my daily to-do list, there are plenty of nights when I finally crawl into bed exhausted but still feeling as if I've accomplished practically nothing. I've scratched the dry cleaner and grocery store off the list, but I haven't done much in terms of life's big-picture items. If this describes a typical day in your life, the good news is that we're not alone.

A 2013 study by Northwestern Mutual Life Insurance found that our fast-paced lifestyle is connected to our inability to make, or stick to, long-term goals. The study showed that a quarter of Americans say they are "often" or "always" too busy to think about their future. Our media-saturated culture isn't exactly helping matters either. Thirty-six percent mentioned their usage of electronic devices. Thirty-one percent of those surveyed said the immediacy of communication through social media and texting was "distracting"—a percentage that increased with each generation. The bad news is that not enough of us are slowing down enough to really reflect on how we want to live our lives. We just seem to be going from one task, one assignment, one errand to the next.

It's crazy, busy times like these that make me think of my grandpa. Pasquale Tomeo was very good at a lot of things. Most important, he was a good father and husband. He was also a great fix-it man and could tweak any runny faucet or broken-down stove or engine and have you back in business in a heartbeat. His tune-up talents were a godsend as he and my grandmother were raising their ten children in a crowded upper flat in Jersey City. When families faced numerous challenges during the depression and then again during World War II, my grandfather was able to turn those talents into real work. Although it was sporadic at times, it helped him take care of his large family.

I was born in Jersey City. So my roots, and in many ways my heart, are still somewhere along the East Coast. But with a growing family, my parents had dreams of raising their children in an area where housing and Catholic school were more affordable and accessible. That dream began to develop into reality when my father was offered a new job opportunity through his older brother, who had settled in at a small engineering firm in the Midwest. So my parents packed up their three daughters and headed to Michigan a few months before my fifth birthday. Every year without fail, we would pile back in the car for the thirteen-hour drive to the East Coast to visit the aunts, uncles, cousins, and Grandma and Grandpa.

While I was growing up in the Detroit area, many children spent summer vacations at cottages along Lakes Huron and Michigan. Or they would take a road trip to Mackinac Island at the tip of the Lower Peninsula and spend the hot summer days munching on the famous Mackinaw Island fudge. When my friends would tell me about what they did for their summer vacations, I don't remember ever feeling at all envious. My parents always turned our road trips into somewhat of an adventure, as much of an adventure as they could be, given that our trips took place in the 1960s and '70s, when DVD players, satellite radio, iPods, and iPhones were not even a blip on the technological horizon. How we survived only the good Lord knows. My nieces and nephews, who can still recall when MTV came into being, look at me as if I'm on drugs when I explain that their mothers and I managed to make it all the way to New Jersey and back again without much more than an AM car radio and actually had fun in the process.

After thinking about my nieces' and nephews' need for gadgets and distractions, I came to understand one of my grandfather's gifts. It's something that in our current frenetic times is frowned upon, dismissed, or in some circles even despised. My grandfather had mastered what the Italians refer to as *l'arte di non fare niente*—"the art of doing nothing," or, more simply put, learning to be still. I can remember arriving in Jersey City and running up the long, dark staircase to my grandparents' apartment. Often I would be greeted by Grandma Tomeo, but not Grandpa. When that was the case, I knew where to look. He would either be down the hall, sitting in his favorite chair, smoking his pipe, and, yes, doing pretty much nothing, or he would be sitting on a bench in the park across the street, where he might be feeding the pigeons or chatting with his friends. For the most part, he was just relaxing and doing nothing other than enjoying the bit of greenery available in the heart of a then very gritty Jersey City.

I wish I could say that being around my grandfather when I was young meant I was soaking up some of his talent for doing nothing. Although I treasured those times, my true appreciation for *l'arte di non fare niente* didn't happen until much later in my life. And when it did, I realized it was a gift not only from my grandfather, but from God. God was working through my grandfather to try and show me that, yes, there really is a need to stop and take a bit of a breather. Or, as one friend of mine often says, "Don't just do something: sit there." Or, as Psalm 46:10 says:

Be still and know that I am God.

When was the last time you actually allowed yourself to just be still, with no distractions from the TV, radio, iPhone, or laptop? There's a beautiful quote from Pope Emeritus Benedict XVI regarding the importance of eliminating the noise and the busyness of our lives in order to hear from God. Benedict made this comment while speaking to young people in his native Germany in 2006, years before the Northwestern Mutual Life study and many other reports on busyness were released:

Put simply, we are no longer able to hear God— there are too many frequencies filling our ears.

If we say we want to hear from God, we need to slow down enough to listen. We are not going to hear

God while moving from task to task attached to the cell phone or planting ourselves in front of the TV for the latest episode of *The Voice* or *Dancing with the Stars*. In the Old Testament, God comes to the Prophet Elijah not in the way one might expect. Since God is all-powerful and knowing, we might assume He would always make a major entrance with thunder and lightning or something else very dramatic and eye catching. Think again:

> Then the Lord said, "Go outside and stand on the mountain before the Lord; the Lord will be passing by." A strong and heavy wind was rending the mountains and crushing rocks before the Lord— but the Lord was not in the wind. After the wind there was an earthquake—but the Lord was not in the earthquake.
>
> After the earthquake there was fire—but the Lord was not in the fire. After the fire there was a tiny whispering sound.
>
> When he heard this, Elijah hid his face in his cloak and went and stood at the entrance of the cave. A voice said to him, "Elijah, why are you here?" (1 Kings 19:11–13)

Blessed Mother Teresa of Calcutta also reminded the world many times that God comes to us in silence:

We cannot find God in noise and agitation. In nature we find silence—the trees, flowers, and grass grow in silence. The stars, the moon, and the sun move in silence. . . . What is essential is not what we say but what God tells us and what He tells others through us. In silence He listens to us. In silence He speaks to our souls. In silence we are granted the privilege of listening to His voice.

I finally began to get the hang of this slowing-down thing when in the summer of 2001 my husband and I took our first pilgrimage to Europe—a trip organized through my parish church. The pilgrimage began in beautiful Salzburg, Austria, and then took us to Venice, Florence, Assisi, and Rome. It involved the church choir, of which my father was an active participant, and meant going back to the land of our ancestors. My husband, who is also Italian American, thought it a great idea to share the trip, especially the Italian portion, with my parents, to learn more about our heritage and to see my father sing in Saint Peter's. Viva Italia! Off we went.

It was a very busy time for me. I was working at a local Christian radio station, hosting my very first talk show, *Christian Talk with Teresa Tomeo*; my communications company was just getting off the ground, and my speaking ministry was beginning to take off.

I was very much looking forward to the trip, but at the same time I was a little worried about the workload I would face when I returned. Little did I know how much my attitude would slowly but eventually change.

It's hard not to fall in love with Italy—it's just so incredibly beautiful. Italy is God showing off and saying "See, lookie what I can do." I honestly don't know how one country not that much bigger than the state of Florida can contain so much stunning scenery. No matter what city or town you're in, there's something new and old to discover around every corner. The churches and buildings date back, in many cases, not just hundreds, but thousands of years and contain incredible mosaics, paintings, and statues. Even in the larger cities, such as Rome and Florence, the apartment balconies are decorated with plants and flowers. Sure, the big cities in Italy have their share of graffiti, garbage issues, and tourist traps, but the good definitely outweighs the bad, and when you have nothing but Italian blood running through your veins, there's an extra connection making the country so attractive. We felt a level of comfort there that we didn't even feel at home.

We're not fluent in Italian by any means. Actually, it was pretty darn embarrassing. We both look very Italian with the dark hair and all the other trimmings common to folks with our heritage, so Italians just started talking to us in Italian. We nodded, smiled, and mumbled a few *prego*s and *grazie*s and tried not to look like total idiots. But what's so great about the Italian people is that they're extremely warm and friendly; once we'd explain that we were Italian American but that our command of their beautiful language was small enough to fit in an espresso cup, they would laugh and do their best to communicate.

Beyond the language issue and the jet lag, no adjusting was needed. We fit right in. And then we realized why. We began to examine the habits of the Italians. In them we saw our own grandparents, especially Grandpa Tomeo. There they were sitting outside, maybe on a small balcony or on a bench by a lovely fountain. The older men were often sitting together in the piazza. It wasn't just the elderly. It seemed that the art of doing nothing was engrained in Italians of all ages.

It's interesting to watch Americans in foreign countries, particularly in Italy, where the pace of life, compared with ours, is in slow motion. Granted, Italians tend to take things to a level of excess. I have several friends who now live and work in Rome. Most of the time they would never trade places, except when they have to go to the bank, pay a utility bill, or hire a repairman. Sometimes the downtime or the art of doing nothing in Italy can be round-the-clock. Nevertheless, we can learn a lot from the Italian way of life. We are so used to flying through the day and not waiting for anything or anyone. We want what we want, and we want it now.

Many of the travelers on that first Italian trip were frustrated with what they perceived to be poor or slow service. Heaven forbid they should have to wait more than ten minutes for a meal. Oh, the injustice of being forced to relax in an outdoor café and having nothing to do but stare at colorful frescoes on the outside of a little church or at some other remarkable structure while you wait for your homemade pasta. What is this world coming to? Someone grab the cell phone and call the Italian version of the Better Business Bureau!

At first my husband and I were admittedly also a bit annoyed with the lackadaisical attitude of most Romans, but eventually we happily settled into the slower pace there. Thankfully, our attitude changed, and now the slower pace is not only something we look forward to on our vacations, whether overseas or at the local beach, but something we have gradually managed to incorporate into our everyday lives.

We realized on that first trip to Italy that slowing down helped us appreciate everything we were experiencing—the food, the wine, the art, the history—that much more. We savored the moment. Most important, the slower pace not only caused us to spend more time looking outward—examining the world around us more closely and appreciating its beauty—it also led to more inward reflection. We gave a lot of thought and prayer to where we were—in the heart of the Catholic Church. We also came away with a better understanding of *who* we were—Christians tracing our spiritual roots and ancestral roots. As Pope Francis explains it in his book *On Heaven and Earth*, being able to look inward can help us heal an interior fracture—a fracture caused by all the distractions in the world:

> What every person must be told is to look inside himself. Distraction is an interior fracture. It will never lead the person to encounter himself for it impedes him from looking into the mirror of his heart. Collecting oneself is the beginning. That is where the dialogue begins. At times, one believes he has the only answer, but that's not the case. I would tell the people of today to seek the experience of entering into the intimacy of their hearts to know the experience, the face of God. That is why I love what Job says after his difficult experience and the dialogues that did not help him in any way: "By hearsay I had heard of you. But now my eyes have

seen you." [Job 42:5] What I tell people is not to know God only by hearing. The Living God is He that you may see with your eyes within your heart.

On the surface, even from a Christian perspective, this concept seems counterproductive. There is so much work to be done in such a hurting world. Aren't we supposed to be the Lord's hands and feet? What about all those references to feeding the hungry and clothing the naked? Jesus insists that if we love Him, we will keep His commandments. We read in James 1:22 that we are supposed to be "doers of the word." Yet we simply will never know exactly what kind of "doing" we're supposed to be undertaking if we don't give ourselves a chance to slow down and hear from God. Too often we get all caught up in the day-to-day details, which can turn into major spiritual roadblocks. I truly believe this is why I've run into so many Mr. and Mrs. Grumpy Pants in both Christian and secular arenas. Some of these types are not exactly fun to be around. Even though only the good Lord knows our inner struggles and what is truly in a person's heart, I do notice a lot of similarities among people who do too much (and tell you of the fact). They are usually the busiest people in the office or the parish, and they're usually the ones putting their noses into everybody's business or ministry effort, wondering why, and often out loud, Sally So-and-So is or isn't doing this or that. They have a solution for everything, and the best solution, if only we knuckleheads would listen, is usually theirs. They just can't seem to relax, even for a minute.

It's important to be able to recognize the difference between being still and laziness. As Pope Francis points out, the art of doing nothing is not an excuse for ignoring responsibilities. It's actually quite the opposite. One of the strongest examples of Jesus explaining the difference between the two is given to us in the New Testament with Jesus's visit to the home of His close friends Martha and Mary. Martha would probably qualify for membership in the Grumpy Pants family, as she is a very busy woman, but a woman who misreads her sister's actions. In Luke 10:38–42, we join Jesus as Martha is busily going about preparing dinner while her sister Mary appears to be doing nothing. Mary, verse 39 tells us, sat at the Lord's feet. And that was so nerve-racking to Martha that she finally had to speak up and put in her two cents.

> Martha, burdened with much serving, came to him and said, "Lord, do you not care that my sister has left me by myself to do the serving? Tell her to help me."

The Lord said to her in reply, "Martha, Martha, you are anxious and worried about many things. There is need of only one thing. Mary has chosen the better part and it will not be taken from her." (Luke 10:40–41)

Jesus is not promoting laziness here or ignoring one's responsibilities. He is saying that everything begins with God, and if we want to hear from God, we have to slow down.

Jesus practiced what He preached. Several passages in the Gospels describe Jesus stepping away from His disciples and the crowds and going off by Himself. The Old Testament also speaks about the benefit of slowing down and learning to be still:

Be still and know that I am God; I will be exalted among the nations. I will be exalted in the earth. (Psalm 46:10)

He leads me beside still waters. He restores my soul. (Psalm 23:2)

But I have calmed and quieted my soul. (Psalm 131:2)

No wonder Jesus lovingly suggests to Martha that all her busyness is not needed, that by being still, Mary has taken the better path. He wasn't just speaking to Martha. Scripture speaks to all of us.

I will be the first one to admit that, despite what I learned on my trip to Italy, slowing down is still a challenge for me. It is extremely hard for me to say no to speaking events—so much so, that I have actually double-booked myself more than once, which is embarrassing, to say the least. Slowly, and ever so slowly, I am learning to pace myself and give myself more time for downtime.

While Christians are called to be *in* the world, not *of* the world, over time we have adopted too many "of the world" characteristics. In 2007, Professor Michael Zigarelli published a five-year "Obstacles to Growth Survey" of data collected from over 20,000 Christians in 139 countries. Zigarelli concluded from this study that

> [t]he accelerated pace and activity level of the modern day distracts us from God and separates us from the abundant, joyful, victorious life He desires for us. . . . [It] may be the case that (1) Christians are assimilating to a culture of busyness, hurry and overload, which leads to (2) God becoming more marginalized in Christians' lives, which leads to (3) a deteriorating relationship with God,

which leads to (4) Christians becoming even more vulnerable to adopting secular assumptions about how to live, which leads to (5) more conformity to a culture of busyness, hurry, and overload. And the cycle begins again.

Zigarelli suggests breaking this constant cycle by reordering our thinking, "including the way we think about who God is and how He wants us to live our lives."

Not only are the sheep too busy for God, so are their shepherds. In the Catholic Church, at least some of this busyness can be attributed to a shortage of priests and a lack of help at the local parish level. The study showed that, by profession, pastors were the most likely to rush from task to task, and that about 65 percent of them felt that their busyness gets in the way of their relationship with God.

Zigarelli's comments remind me of a great quote from Pope John XXII, which for me has turned into a prayer: "Lord this is your Church, not mine. I am tired and going to bed." If Church leaders and Jesus Himself found downtime, don't you think it might be a good practice for us to incorporate?

Knowing that my grandfather was a devout Catholic, I have little doubt that his times with the pigeons and smoking his pipe were also special times of reflection and prayer. In addition to daily Mass, these times served as miniretreats. They allowed him to break away from his ordinary activities as a husband, father, and grandfather and have some moments alone with God.

My grandfather was actually putting his own twentieth-century adaptation on something that dated back to the early Church. In the first few hundred years of Christianity, retreating to the mountains of the desert was greatly admired in the Christian community. The so-called desert fathers, led by Saint Anthony the Great, were a group of hermits settling in the Egyptian desert in the third and fourth centuries A.D. and are considered the founders of monasticism. In the following reflection concerning a life of solitude and interior reflection, Saint Anthony sounds a lot like Pope Francis:

> So like a fish going toward the sea, we must hurry to reach our cell, for fear that if we delay outside we will lose our interior watchfulness.

Given the limited resources of most American immigrants in the early- to mid-twentieth century, escaping to the desert, the mountains, or some other remote part of the world was not even remotely conceivable, but they were wise enough to know they needed to break away. That's what they did in the old country, and they found a way to do it here. To the park, the beach, the local church, or the waterfront they went. For my grandfather, who was raising ten children in a small upper flat in crowded, noisy Jersey City, the park across the street from their apartment building, and right next to the busy Colgate factory, was the closest thing to a place of retreat.

Today, even though there are plenty of Christians who claim they're "too busy" for God, there are those who are learning the art of doing nothing and are heading out to local retreat houses. While it's great to be able to go to a monastery in the mountains, it's not always necessary or possible, especially if you have a family with young children. Most local Catholic dioceses, and Protestant denominations as well, run retreats from a central location or will bring the retreat practically to your front door by conducting it at a local parish or conference center. The length of these retreats varies. Some are conducted over a weekend, others over the course of a day. Others involve just one evening of downtime away from your normal routine. Leaving the world behind even for a few hours can do wonders for our sanity and our soul.

Such retreats are usually centered on a specific topic or theme. I myself have conducted a number of retreats during Lent and Advent—focused on, you guessed it, slowing down and, well, retreating from everyday life.

If you were raised Catholic, think back to the days when you still embraced the annual Lenten practices. The liturgical season was given to us to remind us of Jesus's forty days in the desert. The Catholic Church teaches, as it has for centuries by encouraging prayer and fasting, that Lent is to be viewed and practiced as a kind of extended retreat preparing us for Easter. You might be thinking "Oh, great." This "art of doing nothing" is just one more thing to add to your already-packed schedule. I guess that's one way to look at it, but probably not the most beneficial approach. Surely, allowing yourself to slow down enough to reconnect with God is worth a few minutes a day, a few hours every month, a few days out of the year.

By being like Grandpa and learning *l'arte di non fare niente*, we are giving our bodies and our minds a rest and allowing ourselves to be more open to God. We will never be able to discover God's bucket list for our happiness if we never slow down long enough to hear from Him. So be still. Try it. Just sit there and breathe. Be still, and in a few moments, that flutter in your heart—that sense of relief that washes over you, that state of calm that makes you feel different from how you felt a few minutes before—well, that might just be God sitting and being still with you.

2.

Live Your Passion

When we are whom we are called to be,
we will set the world ablaze.
—Saint Catherine of Siena

If you've ever been in the market to buy a home, you've no doubt heard it said that there are only three things that matter when it comes to property: location, location, location. You spend a great deal of time and effort researching the area and the neighborhood surrounding that house, apartment, or condominium that you've always dreamed of. The search can be exhilarating, but it can also be exhausting. Yet, in the end, feeling safe and secure in your new home lets you settle down and get back to the business of really living your life.

The search for true happiness is a lot like the search for the perfect home. And if you would forgive a play on words, it all comes down to vocation, vocation, vocation. In other words, it all comes down to our sense of purpose. Once we tap into God's calling for our life, it should feel just like home. I like to call it the Goldilocks effect: things aren't too hot or too cold, but just right.

So how would you define *vocation*? According to *Merriam-Webster's*, *vocation* can be defined in a number of ways:

1. A divine call to the religious life.
2. An entry into the priesthood or a religious order.
3. The work in which a person is employed.
4. The special function of an individual or group.

The word *vocation* comes from a Latin term meaning "to call." Finding that call, however, is such a deep desire on our hearts that not only have hundreds of books been written on the topic from both a secular and a religious perspective, but there is also no shortage of people who have found their calling in helping others do the same. A big part of the process is recognizing our gifts and our talents.

Each of us has a special vocation or purpose in life. That vocation is deep in our heart, and finding it is a lot like finding the right home. When we discover it, we experience a sense of peace. But instead of a real estate agent, we need God's help in this search. As the Catechism of the Catholic Church (CCC) reminds us:

The desire for God is written in the human heart, because man is created by God and for God, and God never ceases to draw man to himself. Only in God will he find the truth and happiness he never stops searching for. The dignity of man rests above all on the fact that he is called to communion with God. The invitation to converse with God is addressed to man as soon as he comes into being. For if a man exists it is because God has created him through love, and through love continues to hold him in existence. He cannot live fully according to truth unless he freely acknowledges that love and entrusts himself to his creator. (CCC 27)

But what do we do if we are still searching for God's special call for us in our lives? How do we know that we haven't somehow missed a calling? Is it possible to have more than one calling or vocation? In the Catholic Church, the lifetime commitments made in marriage and Holy Orders (ordination to the priesthood or permanent diaconate) are considered both sacraments and vocations. Motherhood and fatherhood are also considered among the highest callings and take a great deal of sacrifice and dedication. However, moms and dads may also be called to embrace other vocations unique to their gifts and talents. Our vocations may also come to us after having an insight or a strong feeling pulling us in a certain direction. It's different for everyone. It is also a process, according to Blessed Pope John Paul II in his apostolic exhortation "*Christifidelis Laici:* On the Vocation and the Mission of the Lay Faithful." God wants us to find our vocation, to embrace it, and to live it out joyfully:

> In fact, from eternity God has thought of us and has loved us as unique individuals. Every one of us he called by name, as the Good Shepherd "calls his sheep by name" (John 10:3). However, only in the unfolding of the history of our lives and its events is the eternal plan of God revealed to each of us. Therefore it is a gradual process; in a certain sense, one that happens day by day.

That sounds great, but what if we feel like we're alone in a boat and lost at sea? What do we do if we're still searching for God's call in our life and that horizon is nowhere in sight? How do we know our inner compass is working correctly and that we haven't lost our way? And do we know we won't suffer the same fate as Saint Peter in his attempt to walk on water?

> During the fourth watch of the night, [Jesus] came toward them, walking on the sea.

When the disciples saw him walking on the sea they were terrified. "It is a ghost," they said, and they cried out in fear.

At once he spoke to them, "Take courage, it is I; do not be afraid."

Peter said to him in reply, "Lord, if it is you, command me to come to you on the water."

He said, "Come."

Peter got out of the boat and began to walk on the water toward Jesus. But when he saw how strong the wind was he became frightened, and, beginning to sink, he cried out, "Lord, save me!"

Immediately Jesus stretched out his hand and caught him, and said to him, "O you of little faith, why did you doubt?"

After they got into the boat, the wind died down. Those who were in the boat did him homage, saying, "Truly, you are the Son of God." (Matthew 14:25–33)

Trouble came Saint Peter's way when he took his eyes off Christ to look at the wind. Here's where prayerful discernment comes in. Discernment, according to *Merriam-Webster's*, is "the quality of being able to grasp and comprehend what is obscure." In the secular realm, we discern important decisions pretty regularly. We discern whether a particular investment is the best place for our money. We discern whether someone might be a good business partner. These decisions take some due diligence on our part. We have to do some homework and take time for some serious thinking. Prayerful discernment brings God into the process. We ask Him to help us be open to what He might be calling us to do. It's obviously not easy to make sure we are charting the correct course, but just as in other decisions we turn to those we trust for input and advice, who better to help us determine our vocation than the ultimate vocation director Himself?

One real-life example of turning to God for help in finding our vocation is played out regularly in the "Careers Through Faith" seminars conducted by Nick Synko of Synko & Associates, a career consulting firm based in Ann Arbor, Michigan. Don't let the title of these seminars fool you. They're not necessarily about finding a new vocation within the Catholic Church or a specific Christian community. As Nick Synko explains, they're about tapping into our faith to discover our vocation. He helps participants look at their lives a bit differently to really understand, discover, or perhaps even rediscover their vocation.

It's a mindset. Some people look at life as a destination someday to be achieved and everything until then is a to-do task. Others live daily the journey of serving others and therefore serve the Lord. When you are on the "journey mindset," you routinely find fulfilling experiences to serve others, provided you are working within your purpose or mission. A well-lived life is a daily thing.

And, as Blessed Pope John Paul II once explained, there are some important steps we can take to help us discover our godly vocation:

To be able to discover the actual will of the Lord in our lives always involves the following: a receptive listening to the Word of God and the Church, fervent and constant prayer, recourse to a wise and loving spiritual guide, and a faithful discernment of the gifts and talents given by God as well as the diverse social and historical situations in which one lives.

For me, "receptive listening to the Word of God" translates into really paying attention to all the readings during Mass. It also helps me to arrive a little bit early, to give myself a few minutes to settle down and leave the world behind. My spiritual director also advised me a long time ago to actually take time to pray with the readings before Mass so the words of Scripture can really penetrate.

"Fervent and constant prayer" is another way of saying "Put everything at the foot of the cross." The Catholic Church has the beautiful practice of Eucharistic adoration, in the which the Blessed Sacrament—Jesus in the Eucharist—is exposed and adored in either a church or a separate chapel. The "adoration" can be done by just sitting or kneeling quietly before Jesus. Think of it as a quiet time with God. Some like to recite the Rosary silently. Others find it helpful to read Scripture. Adoration is a good exercise, because we have to make a real effort to carve out time in our busy day for it.

To come to the "faithful discernment of the gifts and talents given by God" and to have "recourse to a wise and loving spiritual guide," talking to those we trust can help us understand ourselves a little bit better and determine whether our vocation compass is pointed in the right direction.

Sometimes we might confuse a skill for a talent. A skill—such as being a whiz at handling the family's finances—can certainly be useful. But if that skill feels more like a chore, you can bet that numbers aren't going to make you happy. You can also bet that this isn't your gift or talent. Career counselors such as Nick Synko will tell you that skills shouldn't be totally tossed aside, for they can be constructive in helping you achieve your goals. However, skills are not what you need to tap into if joy and happiness are your end game.

I was very good at reporting, but after a while it felt as if I were on a TV/radio news assembly line, just cranking out one sensational and meaningless story after another. I still had the writing, research, and storytelling abilities, but applying those skills in this way no longer brought me any sense of fulfillment or accomplishment. I still loved communications. I just had to pray for discernment in figuring out how to use these skills and talents differently. It took time, but with God at the center of the process, I was able to find my true purpose as a Catholic evangelist, communicator, and motivational speaker.

The role of God in our search for our true vocation, our search for God's bucket list, is beautifully illustrated by Pope Emeritus Benedict XVI in an apostolic letter initiating a Year of Faith beginning in October 2012. In this letter, titled *Porta Fide* ("Door of Faith," from Acts 14:27), he writes that to enter through the door of faith "is to set out on a journey that lasts a lifetime."

Perhaps we are cradle Catholics who received the sacraments as children but have done little or nothing with our faith since then except perhaps going to Mass, but we are now trying to get some sense of how God fits into the bigger scheme of things. Or perhaps we are Christians who made a major commitment to Christ years ago but haven't done much to nurture the relationship or dine with Christ, yet we are still hoping for some direction. Or maybe we have been wandering online or searching through the local bookstore—looking for, as Pope Emeritus Benedict puts it in *Porta Fidei*, "the ultimate meaning and definitive truth of [our] lives and of the world."

Benedict further writes in this letter:

> We must rediscover a taste for feeding ourselves on the Word of God, faithfully handed down by the Church. . . . Indeed, the teaching of Jesus still resounds in our day with the same power: "Do not labor for the food which perishes, but for the food which endures to eternal life" (John 6:27). The question posed by his listeners is the same that we ask today: "What must we do, to be doing the works of God?" (John 6:28). We know Jesus's reply: "This is the work of God that you believe in him whom he has sent" (John 6:29). Belief in Jesus Christ, then, is the way to arrive definitively at salvation."

As a motivational speaker, I like to leave my audiences with an action plan or take-away practices that can help them stay focused on their relationship with God and where He is leading them. Here are a few ideas for those on the lookout for the Lord's bucket list. (You'll also find more details on how to apply these activities to your daily life in our resource list in the back of this book.)

- Daily prayer
- Scripture reading
- Self reflection (jotting down dreams, goals, and what makes you feel most peaceful and productive, then taking this list to prayer)
- Input from a mentor or a spiritual director

And last but not least on this bucket list would be a pat on the back—being encouraged by the mere fact that you're on your way. Maybe you don't quite know where that way is leading, but that's okay too.

Blessed Mother Teresa of Calcutta had a great saying that I use to close many of my presentations with—to encourage my audience to at least give whatever they're working on in their lives the old college try. Mother Teresa's words certainly apply to the content of my talks, many of which are designed to help Catholics and other Christians engage the culture, better understand their faith, and improve the spiritual environment in their homes. These words are also very applicable to searching for God's will in our lives—our true calling:

God doesn't expect us to be successful; only faithful.

And by earnestly seeking God's direction in our lives, we are being faithful. We don't lose sight of the deep desire to someday find that vocation. God willing, when we get there we will set the world on fire. As the great Saint Catherine of Siena reminds us:

Be who you were meant to be and you will set the world on fire.

In the meantime, who knows how many sparks we will ignite and how much joy we will find in the journey? As Blessed John Henry Newman wrote of this journey:

God has created me to do Him some definite service; He has committed some work to me which He has not committed to another. I have my mission— I may never know it in this life, but I shall be told it in the next.

Somehow I am necessary for His purposes. . . . I have a part in a great work, I am a link in a chain, a bond of connection between persons.

3.

Live with Instruction

 Trust in the Lord with all of your heart and
lean not on your own understanding.
—Proverbs 3:5–6

I am sure that growing up, many of you had the experience of watching your parents attempt to put together one of your precious Christmas gifts. Do the words "some assembly required" ring a bell? How difficult could assembling a bike or that Barbie dollhouse really be? Directions? I don't need stinking directions. Several frustrating hours later, your parents are still scratching their heads staring in utter confusion at the pile of parts in front of them. Finally they decide to give in and grab for the manual buried at the bottom of the box.

Our approach to life is a lot like that. We are given such solid, reliable, and helpful directions from God and His witnesses on the best way to navigate through this world. But rarely do we ever read these directions or take them seriously. How difficult could this happiness thing be, after all? We're mature, educated, intelligent adults living in the most modern and sophisticated country in the world. Unlike our parents and grandparents, most of us have at least a high school diploma and one college degree, if not several, so the temptation is to think we have everything we need to navigate the highways and byways of life. And, let's be honest, don't a lot of us think that relying too much on God and His word in the Bible is sometimes seen as fanatical?

Well, when I found my life to be like that pile of parts on the living room floor, that's when I decided to stop worrying about whether I might be seen as fanatical and started taking a look at the best instruction manual around.

A former pastor of mine, Father Richard Steiber, really helped me move forward in appreciating the Bible. Father Steiber was larger than life even though he was just over five feet tall. What this wonderful priest lacked in height he made up in enthusiasm. He looked so small as he stood at the foot of the altar with the huge crucifix hanging on the wall behind him. His actions and his words, however, had the power to quickly transform him into a giant of a witness for the Gospel. He would walk up and down the very long aisle of our very large parish with the Bible in hand. He insisted we think of the word *Bible* as an acronym for "Basic Instructions Before Leaving

Earth." The first time I heard him say this, my husband and I were what you might call C&E Catholics: Christmas and Easter Catholics. We made it to Mass on holidays and a few times in between. But despite our weak worship practices, Father Steiber's words never left us. It took years of pain, trial, and error, but we eventually did come to realize that the Bible, along with the Catechism of the Catholic Church, papal encyclicals, and other Church writings now easily available online or in bookstores are really filled with beautiful and very necessary directions—directions that are key in building a God-centered life.

The Catechism of the Catholic Church drives this point home and is explicit about the need for Scripture in our lives:

> For this reason the Church has always venerated the Scriptures as she venerates the Lord's Body. She never ceases to present to the faithful the bread of life, taken from the one table of God's Word and God's body.
>
> In Sacred Scripture the Church constantly finds her nourishment and her strength, for she welcomes it not as a human word, "but as what it really is: the word of God." In the sacred books, the Father who is in heaven comes lovingly to meet His children and talks with them. (CCC 103, 104)

To say it another way, the Bible is not something to be left on the bookshelf or coffee table. The Bible is the Word of God, and it is to be taken seriously, not lightly as a hobby or an extracurricular activity.

The Catechism of the Catholic Church states:

"And such is the force and power of the Word of God that it can serve the Church as her support and vigor, and the children of the Church as strength for their faith, food for the soul, and a pure and lasting fount of spiritual life." Hence "access to Sacred Scripture ought to be open wide to the Christian faithful."

Therefore, the study of the sacred page should be the very soul of sacred theology. The ministry of the Word, too—pastoral preaching, catechetics and all forms of Christian instruction, among which the liturgical homily should hold pride of place—is healthily nourished and thrives in holiness through the Word of Scripture.

The Church "forcefully and specifically exhorts all the Christian faithful . . . to learn the surpassing knowledge of Jesus Christ, by frequent reading of the divine Scriptures. Ignorance of the Scriptures is ignorance of Christ." (CCC 131–133)

How many of us say we believe in God but have never really made an effort to read the Bible? I'm asking this question based on my own life experience. I always said I believed in God, but my actions proved otherwise. We always had a Bible in our home growing up, and the same held true for me and my husband, Dominick. We received a beautiful Bible as one of our wedding gifts. But it was for the most part a coffee-table book. That's kind of sad, isn't it? To say you believe in something or someone, but then for the most part ignore a major source of that belief? If you love someone and want to be in a relationship with them, you need to get to know them better and to spend time with them. In the twenty-first century we have myriad ways to get to know one another better. In addition to spending face time together, we talk on the cell phone or skype. We e-mail, text, post, and tweet. We don't seem to have any trouble taking time to see what is on the mind of our current person of interest or BFF—Best Friend Forever. Yet, for many of us, God is at the bottom of our communication list. This is not healthy for anybody. If our relationship with God breaks down, we can easily get lost, dazed, and confused, and then our lives resemble the pieces of that bike or dollhouse on the living room floor Christmas morning.

Just ask the folks over at the Pew Forum on Religion & Public Life. The Pew Center's "U.S. Religious

Knowledge Survey," released in the fall 2010, was a perfect example of how little Christians know about their own religion. On this survey, atheists, Mormons, and Jews—not Christians—scored highest on this quiz, which included questions concerning the core teachings, history, and leading figures of major world religions. More than four in ten, or about 45 percent, of Catholics questioned had no idea of what really happens at Communion. They didn't realize that the bread and wine are not merely symbols of Christ but actually become the body and blood of Christ. How is that possible when the Eucharist is considered the source and summit of the Catholic faith? Yes, in part we can put some of the blame on teachers, for many of us grew up with little more than a case of butterflies, banners, and balloons in religion class. But the blame game only goes so far. In the end we are responsible for our own salvation.

We're also responsible for properly developing our conscience to help us make important normal decisions. Blessed John Henry Cardinal Newman, a nineteenth-century English convert to Catholicism, and considered a major influence on Christianity and the culture in his country, wrote: "Conscience has rights because it has duties." And he wasn't just talking about a duty to keep me, myself, and I happy. He was talking about the duty to choose wisely and carefully, to discern right from wrong. And that gets us back to where we started. It is so easy to become clouded by our own poor or absentminded thinking and lack of instruction that we often act as if there is no more black and white, only gray. We pick and choose what we want to do according to our own personal needs and desires, without thinking about how our decisions might impact others close to us or even society at large.

Archbishop Charles J. Chaput, then archbishop of Denver, said in a 2009 address to the Catholic Physicians' Guild that that type of approach might help us sleep a little better at night, but it is not going to fly with God.

> God will demand an accounting. As individuals, we can claim to believe whatever we want. But God knows our hearts better than we do. If we don't conform our hearts and actions to the faith we claim to believe, we're simply fooling ourselves.

The archbishop's comments reflect the information in the "Obstacles to Growth" and "U.S. Religious Knowledge" surveys mentioned earlier and should be a reminder for us that even those filling up the churches on Sunday do not necessarily have a solid grasp of what following God really means.

People often tell me I am preaching to the choir when broadcasting on Catholic radio or speaking in Catholic and Protestant churches. My response is often "Have you heard the choir lately?" Besides, I explain, every choir needs practice if it is going to stay in tune. And while people listening to Catholic media or attending faith-related events might be more interested in their faith than the average person, it doesn't guarantee they are in full communion with the Church or even understand the need to be.

I can attest to the fact that being a Catholic Christian means a lot more than just calling yourself something and showing up for Church once in a while. That was the case with my own journey back to God and the Church. Joining a Bible study group was a significant step for both my husband and me in developing a much deeper relationship with Christ— and, to tell the truth, with each other. Dominick was the first to say yes to an invitation to a men's Bible study group. At that point in our lives, about eight years into our marriage, we had become very distant from each other, consumed by our careers and spending less and less time at home. When we did see each other, much of our time was spent arguing about household responsibilities, money issues, and the lack of time together. We were both responsible for the rift in the relationship, but we did a lot more finger-pointing than looking in the mirror. As Dominick will tell you, his yes came more out of desperation than desire. We were married in the Catholic Church and were enrolled as a married couple at the local parish in suburban Detroit, and now we were wondering why our relationship had almost come to a crashing halt. What did we expect to happen when we left the driver's manual and, frankly, *the driver* back at the ultimate repair shop? We didn't think we needed any help, instructions, or directions of any kind to find our way home or put the pieces of our lives back together.

Something deep down told Dominick—obviously the Holy Spirit—that he, or both of us, needed this Bible study group. The last time he and I had looked at a Bible was during our wedding preparation. And, if I remember correctly, technically we didn't even actually look at or pick up the Bible and open it. Back then, if someone would have asked me, I doubt whether I could have named the authors of the four Gospels. We were poorly instructed Catholics who knew little about the Church and even less about Scripture.

I'm going to shine the spotlight on Archbishop Chaput one more time. He has given a number of sobering talks in recent years on the sorry state of catechesis, or religious instruction, in North America. During a presentation to a catechetical congress in British Columbia in 2010, Chaput reminded his audience that those who forget history—in this case, biblical history—are doomed to repeat it.

> What's happening today in the Church is not a "new" story. We find it repeated throughout the Old Testament. It took very little time for the Hebrews to start worshipping a golden calf. Whenever the people of God grew too prosperous or comfortable, they forgot where they came from. They forgot their God, because they no longer thought it was important to teach about him. Because they failed to catechize, they failed to inoculate themselves against the idolatries in their surrounding cultures. And eventually, they began praying to the same alien gods as the pagans among whom they lived.

Unfortunately we are, Chaput said, repeating history.

> We have the same struggles today. Instead of changing the culture around us, we Christians have allowed ourselves to be changed by the culture. We've compromised too cheaply. We've hungered

after assimilating and fitting in. And in the process, we've been bleached out and absorbed by the culture we were sent to make holy.

And that's why Christians, both Catholic and Protestant, find the directions too overwhelming. Because there has been so much bleaching and absorbing, they don't know who to believe. Not only has the culture possibly filled their heads with all sorts of crazy ideas contrary to the basic tenets of the Christian faith, our society gives a big thumbs-down when it comes to religious authority.

Why should we believe the pope, and the other leaders of the Church? Aren't they just fallible men like the rest of us? What about the horrible sexual-abuse scandals in the priesthood and all the corrupt Church leaders over the centuries? What about all those rich televangelists who were living double lives? Are these "directions" really reliable, considering the source? Who died and put those guys in charge anyway?

Well, God did, to be quite blunt about it. For example, the history of the Catholic Church dates back two thousand years. Jesus founded the Catholic Church and entrusted it to Saint Peter and the apostles. After His death, resurrection, and ascension, He left Peter and the apostles in the good hands of the third person of the Trinity, the Holy Spirit, who He promised would guide them in all truth:

> But when he comes, the Spirit of truth, he will guide you to all truth. He will not speak on his own, but he will speak what he hears, and will declare to you the things that are coming. (John 16:13)

Today, however, it's understandable how people's trust in the Church and her teachings has weakened when some of those responsible for passing on those teachings have caused so much pain and humiliation through sexual abuse. Or perhaps you were hurt in some other way by a priest or a lay minister? These are issues the Church will always need to recognize and address. As a Catholic talk show host, I receive all kinds of e-mails from Catholics across the country who feel they have been greatly wronged by their parish priest or deacon. Being a very public person in the Church, I will spare you the details, but I have my own battle scars.

What keeps me going is Jesus and the truth of Church teaching. Is what the Church teaches true? I can honestly say that I regularly see Church teachings backed up by secular research. Whether it has to do with the fallout from abortion, contraception, or sexual promiscuity, the Church is proved right over and over again. That doesn't mean that clergy and other Church officials don't sin. It does mean, as explained in the Catechism, that there is no error in the teachings, because those teachings come from the Church through the intercession of the Holy Spirit:

> "The Roman Pontiff, head of the college of bishops, enjoys this infallibility in virtue of his office, when, as supreme pastor and teacher of all the faithful . . . he proclaims by a definitive act a doctrine pertaining to faith or morals. . . . The infallibility promised to the Church is also present in the body of bishops when, together with Peter's successor, they exercise the supreme Magisterium," above all in an Ecumenical Council. When the Church through its supreme Magisterium proposes a doctrine "for belief as being divinely revealed," and as the teaching of Christ, the definitions "must be adhered to with the obedience of faith." This infallibility extends as far as the deposit of divine Revelation itself. (CCC 891)

My pastor and spiritual director, Monsignor Michael Bugarin of the Archdiocese of Detroit, is always telling me "all things Christ." Certainly he is referring to major moral issues. As Christians, we need to follow the Church teachings and what the Scriptures teach us, not only about such major matters as the sacredness of life from womb to tomb and the dignity of the human person made in the image and likeness of God, but also in the not-so-heavy issues. Our faith should guide us in day-to-day matters as well.

I was surprised to learn that the Catholic Church gives directions for every area of our lives, including family, work, education, the arts, music, science, the environment, and even sports. That's right. In 2004, Blessed Pope John Paul II instituted a "Church and Sport" section within the Pontifical Council for the Laity. And in 2010, Pope Emeritus Benedict XVI launched the John Paul II Foundation for Sport with the focus of building spiritual character through excellence in sporting skills and fitness. Or, as the Catholic convert and well-known apologist Steve Ray says, we can go to the optometrist and get a prescription for a new pair of glasses so we can see the world from a truly Catholic perspective.

But how do we do that, and where do we begin?

For my husband and me, Bible study was the very first step in opening our eyes and our hearts to a completely different worldview and way of life. I enrolled in a women's Bible study group about two years after my husband began studying Scripture. We then joined a couple's course. At that time, in the Archdiocese of Detroit and elsewhere around the country, Catholic Bible studies were not nearly as available as they are today. We were in the early '90s then, and so we found ourselves studying Scripture within a Protestant format. We will be forever grateful for the experience and for the friends we made along the way, both Catholic and Protestant, who encouraged us in our journey. However, as we continued to go to Mass, receive the sacraments, and get more involved in our local parish, we noticed that something was missing in the Protestant Bible study. For obvious reasons, there was no teaching concerning the Eucharist, the Blessed Mother, and the saints, despite the many Scripture verses pertaining to these subjects. They weren't part of Protestant theology, so they weren't up for discussion.

Another thing that kept us Catholic was that Protestants are open to personal interpretation of Scripture. But everyone couldn't be correct. Some Protestants believe in infant baptism; some don't. Some believe in a type of salvation called "once saved, always saved"; some don't. Some believe in the saints; some don't. The personal interpretation of Scripture and disagreements over how to apply Scripture were troubling to us, and in the end, we found it too confusing to weed out one denomination from the next. (At the time we were on our way back to the Catholic Church, there were at least thirty-four thousand Protestant denominations.)

Also, in 1994, the Church had released the English translation of The Catechism of the Catholic Church, which helped to clarify and confirm the importance of the proper interpretation of Scripture:

> Read the Scripture within "the living Tradition of the whole Church." According to a saying of the Fathers, Sacred Scripture is written principally in the Church's heart rather than in documents and records, for the Church carries in her Tradition the living memorial of God's Word, and it is the Holy Spirit who gives her the spiritual interpretation of the Scripture ("... according to the spiritual meaning which the Spirit grants to the Church").
>
> Be attentive to the analogy of faith. By "analogy of faith" we mean the coherence of the truths of faith among themselves and within the whole plan of Revelation. (CCC 113–114)

Another event that did much to once again confirm my choice to stay in the Catholic Church was an e-mail exchange I had with one of my listeners. Her line of thinking showed what happens when we rely on personal interpretation without proper guidance. She reminded me a lot of myself as a cradle Catholic. I once thought, as she still did, that when it comes to making moral decisions concerning voting and other important actions, as long as one takes a few minutes to pray about them and in one's own mind is fine with those choices, then one is also fine with God. But I would eventually come to understand, through a series of crucial steps worth reiterating here, that there is, or should be, much more involved than just one's own individual opinion. I felt I had an awful lot to be thankful for, and I wanted to show my gratitude to God for saving my marriage by getting to know Him better. I began by getting myself back to Mass. I then enrolled in a Bible study. Both of these steps lit a fire in me to know even more, and my husband and I began to study our Catholic faith. All these efforts were key in helping me overcome my own faulty thinking and faulty ways of living. I was hoping my e-mail exchange with this young woman might encourage her to do the same.

She described herself as a former TV producer with a college degree and twelve years of Catholic education. This woman, who was now a stay-at-home mom, contacted me after some discussions on my radio show on the proper formation of conscience—in particular, on helping Catholics understand their responsibility at the voting booth. Catholic radio apostolates are not allowed to endorse candidates outright. We are called though to help our listeners understand the issues from a Catholic worldview. Our Catholic faith, after all, should be not just *a* factor when we go into the voting booth, but *the* factor. Christians are called to love God with their whole heart, mind, and strength. No fence sitting. She was very pleasant, but also very proud and not as well informed as she thought regarding Catholicism and hot-button election issues, including abortion, about which she claimed to be very concerned. She said her mind was already made up, even though her opinion was in stark opposition to Scripture and Church teaching. According to this young woman, she had used her media background to "research" the issues. She had thought and prayed hard, and her "conscience" had guided her to these various conclusions.

"Surely then," I responded, "that means you also followed the steps for proper formation of conscience laid out in paragraphs 1783 through 1785 in the Catechism?" In these paragraphs the Catechism states:

Conscience must be informed and moral judgment enlightened. A well-formed conscience is upright and truthful. It formulates its judgments according to reason, in conformity with the true good willed by the wisdom of the Creator. The education of conscience is indispensable for human beings who are subjected to negative influences and tempted by sin to prefer their own judgment and to reject authoritative teachings.

The education of the conscience is a lifelong task. From the earliest years, it awakens the child to the knowledge and practice of the interior law recognized by conscience. Prudent education teaches virtue; it prevents or cures fear, selfishness and pride, resentment arising from guilt, and feelings of complacency, born of human weakness and faults. The education of the conscience guarantees freedom and engenders peace of heart.

In the formation of conscience the Word of God is the light for our path, we must assimilate it in faith and prayer and put it into practice. We must also examine our conscience before the Lord's Cross. We are assisted by the gifts of the Holy Spirit, aided by the witness or advice of others and guided by the authoritative teaching of the Church. (CCC 1783–1785)

Well, at least she was honest. She wrote back and divulged that she didn't even own a Catechism and wasn't aware of what the Church actually taught about formation of conscience, especially the part about being aided by "the witness or advice of others" and "the authoritative teachings of the Church." Nor had she read some of the other documents I had rec-

ommended, including those that addressed the issues she felt were up for discussion and debate. Her
research was limited to secular sources that were
closely aligned with her political views.

I had no doubt that this listener had taken the matter to prayer, but if after our time with God, we walk
away with something not in line with the Church and
His word, then a few bells should go off somewhere,
and we should have the courage, as this woman
eventually did, to admit that "Houston, we have a
problem." Otherwise, as Archbishop Chaput said in
British Columbia, we are saying we know more than
God, the pope, and two thousand years of teaching:

> If we're embarrassed about Church teachings, or
> if we disagree with them, or if we've decided that
> they're just too hard to live by, or too hard to ex-
> plain, then we've already defeated ourselves.

As Catholics, we look at Scripture, sacred tradi-
tion, and the Magisterium (the teaching authority
of the Church) as a three-legged stool—no one of
them can stand alone, isolated from the other two.
Although our journey back into relationship with
Christ began in a Protestant Bible study group, we
never thought it made any sense to abandon the
church Christ founded in order to rediscover Him.

Somehow, someway, we knew He was there in the Catholic Church, and in the most profound way: in the real presence of the Eucharist. At that point it was certainly not head knowledge, but knowledge in our hearts and, I believe, the grace of the sacraments beginning to take root.

If the Eucharist is really what the Church says—the body of Christ—then why would anyone leave? This is basically what Saint Peter said to Jesus after a number of His disciples walked away. Jesus had just given what we referenced earlier—the Eucharistic discourse. He explained that He was the bread of life come down from heaven. Well, it was just too much information for some. They thought it was a "hard" teaching and left. Not Saint Peter. The Holy Spirit led him to believe that truly there was no place else to go:

> Many of his disciples returned to their former way of life and no longer accompanied him. Jesus then said to the Twelve, "Do you also want to leave?" Simon Peter answered him, "Master, to whom shall we go? You have the words of eternal life. We have come to believe and are convinced that you are the Holy One of God." (John 6:66–69)

Like Saint Peter, there were plenty of times when Dominick and I stumbled. We fell down and got up, and we did this more than once. Most important, we were just hungry to find out more about God, and we kept reaching out desperately for the directions. The more we read Scripture and got involved in parish ministries, the more we wanted to know. Eventually Catholic evangelism began to explode. EWTN (the Eternal Word Television Network, www.ewtn .com) was gaining in popularity and helping to develop a new media called Catholic radio. Catholic apologetics ministries, including Catholic Answers (www.catholic.com) began to publicly challenge anti-Catholicism and fundamentalism. Catholic Bible studies were also being formed, so we left our Protestant study group behind and dove into Catholic Scripture studies, among other resources. Again, we will be forever grateful for that first invitation made to my husband by a Protestant brother. God used him as a vehicle to help us find our way home.

Years later, when my husband was close to earning his master's degree in pastoral ministry and I was well on my way into developing my speaking and writing ministry, I had the blessing of speaking at a conference alongside one of the Church's most prominent and popular speakers and Bible scholars, Dr. Scott Hahn. Scott is a convert to Catholicism. At that conference, he told attendees, "Catholics are sitting on Fort Knox, and we don't even know it." When

Dominick and I started to understand what was available to us in the Church—the Scripture, the sacraments, the saints, the teachings—we thought, *Why haven't we heard or read any of this before?* Along the way, we would hear the same comments expressed by many other "reverts," as we call ourselves. We would also come to understand that while our instructors in the faith, laity or religious, were partly to blame, we were also culpable, and in a larger way. It goes back to choices. You and I make some good ones and some bad ones. And in the end, as Blessed Mother Teresa of Calcutta says regarding other people, "This is between you and God. It was never between you and them anyway."

Spending more time with the Bible, and less time with the laptop or TV, is a major part of a very necessary pop-culture detox. This change can be a big benefit, not only for you, but for your whole family. In 1999, the American Academy of Pediatrics issued a policy statement insisting there should be "no TV for children two years old and younger." The AAP has good reason for its concern, which is based on a growing body of evidence showing the impact of television on a child's rapidly developing brain. In 2011, the AAP modified the policy statement, but only slightly. Because of the rapid growth of computer technology over the last ten years or so, the organization was aware that most households contained several computers, TVs, and other electronic gadgets. Keeping toddlers completely away from screen exposure was probably not realistic. Nevertheless, the AAP maintains that television, computers, and babies don't mix. For those in grade school and high school, they suggest no more than two hours of TV a day. However, a 2010 Kaiser Family Foundation study—"Generation M2: Media in the Lives of 8- to 18-Year-Olds"—found that tweens and teens are consuming fifty-three hours of media a week; most of those hours are still in front of the television set.

The thought of telling your spouse or your children that they need to join you in your efforts to unplug from the world and reconnect with God may make you want to rush to the nearest Rite Aid with a Xanax prescription. Don't panic! Back out of the Rite Aid parking lot. Step out of the vehicle and go back into the house—or, better yet, to church. Instead of grabbing for the anxiety medication, grab for the directions instead. I know what you're about to say: "Give me a break. Okay. I know we have the Bible and the Catechism. But so you mean to tell me the Church actually has advice available to help families deal with texting, sexting, Tweeting, and all things media?" And my response is a big "You betcha, and wait, there is even so much more," as that quirky "amazing Ginsu knife" ad used to proclaim. When the Catholic Church claims to contain the fullness of truth, she means it; and, by golly, we don't have to be another Dr. Scott Hahn or Steve Ray to make sense of the Church's wisdom.

A paperback copy of the Catechism is still only about ten bucks—talk about a worthwhile investment! Every Catholic should have the Bible and the Catechism within reach. It will help you get used to reading the directions. It is a matter of personal preference in terms of the translation but we use the RSV or Revised Standard Version. But find the Bible that best works for you. I would suggest visiting your local Catholic bookstore or ask for some suggestions from your parish priest.

Some of my favorite media-related documents are the World Communications Day statements written by the pope and released yearly on January 24, the feast day of Saint Francis de Sales—the patron saint of writers and journalists. These statements are fairly short, only two to three pages max, yet they're filled with practical nuggets about media in the lives of everyday Catholics. In the last few years of his papacy, Pope Emeritus Benedict XVI used these statements to write and teach about life in the digital age. One of these statements, given to us by Blessed Pope John Paul II in 2004, was titled "The Media and the

Family: A Risk and a Richness." In it, John Paul called for much of what medical and psychological experts cite as absolutely necessary when it comes to trying to raise a family in such a media-saturated culture—*moderation*. I always find it so affirming as well as fascinating how in every area of our lives the Church teachings are repeatedly proven to be true. The very sound advice from the "professional experts" as we point out here echoes what the Church teaches.

Remember that popular phrase popping up on T-shirts and wristbands in the late '90s—"What would Jesus do?" Well, the pope's World Communications Day statements give us the answers as to what Jesus would watch, listen to, read, and search for online. And, no, you don't have to fly over to the Eternal City and get a special visitor's pass to the Vatican Library to find these and other Church documents. Just put "World Communications Day statements" into any search engine and, Eureka!, you'll have more than enough information to become your own Catholic media activist group.

Now for Bible study: If you feel a bit insecure or intimated about going to a study group, don't worry. You can read the Bible in the privacy of your own home, at the office, on a park bench, or anywhere in between. Daily devotionals are available online or in paperback. And, yep, there are apps for devotionals

as well. Many parishes post links to the daily readings on the home page of their websites. We also have
a number of great Bible study links in our resource
section. Frankly, there is just no excuse not to study
the Bible. Some of my favorite resources include the
following:

- The Magnificat: www.magnificat.net
- Word Among Us: www.wau.org
- Living Faith: www.livingfaith.com
- One Bread, One Body: www.presentation
  ministries.com

But don't rule out a Bible study group. It's often
very helpful to get the perspective of other Catholics,
and part of the wonderment of this journey is that
we're not alone. We are all part of the body of Christ.
After we left Protestant studies, my husband continued his scriptural education at Sacred Heart Major
Seminary in Detroit. I decided to sign up for Bible
study at Catholic Scripture Study (www.cssprogram
.net), and I enjoyed it so much, I continued with it for
several years. Most of such Scripture study programs
have everything you need for offering Bible study in
a class setting. They come complete with questions
and study guides, as well as a DVD lecture on each
section given by noted Scripture scholars and com-

mentators. Don't let your lack of Bible knowledge keep you away. Everyone has to start somewhere, and most of those who sign up for these classes are, or were at some point, just like you. They're hungry to know more about their God and their Church. Most important, they're humble enough to ask for directions. And, getting back to the wise and wonderful words of Archbishop Chaput, we need to practice what we preach.

We need to really believe what we claim to believe. We need to stop calling ourselves "Catholic" if we don't stand with the Church in her teachings—all of them. But if we really *are* Catholic, or at least if we *want* to be, then we need to act like it with obedience and zeal and a fire for Jesus Christ in our hearts. God gave us the faith in order to share it. This takes courage. It takes a deliberate dismantling of our own vanity. When we do that, the Church is strong. When we don't, she grows weak. It's that simple.

In a culture of confusion, the Church is our only reliable guide. So let's preach and teach our Catholic beliefs with passion. And let's ask God to make us brave enough and humble enough to follow our faith to its radical conclusions.

4.

Live in the Mess

I walked a mile with Pleasure
She chatted all the way,
But left me none the wiser
For all she had to say.
I walked a mile with Sorrow
And ne'er a word said she;
But oh, the things I learned from her
When Sorrow walked with me!
—Robert Browning Hamilton

Thanks much, Mr. Hamilton. You're quite an eloquent wordsmith, but if walking with sorrow and suffering is such a good idea, then why is our first reaction to run as fast as possible in the opposite direction? I think we all know the answer to that question: we're human. Even Jesus—the Alpha and the Omega, the beginning and the end—on the night before His crucifixion asked His Father to remove the cup of suffering He knew He was about to endure.

> Father, if you are willing, take this cup away from me; still, not my will but yours be done. (Luke 22:42)

So we're in excellent company when it comes to wanting to avoid the messiness of life. But if Jesus hadn't said yes to the mess of an excruciatingly painful, horrible, and humiliating death on the cross, where would we be? As the old saying goes, there really is no Easter Sunday without Good Friday. Suffering was okay for Jesus, because although He was fully human, He is also God. He could handle the rough stuff and then some. For you and me, it's much easier to read about the cross in our daily devotionals or be reminded of the Lord's sacrifice during Holy Week homilies. We can close the Bible or walk out after Mass and put the message of the suffering servant back on the shelf.

Let's face it. A lot of us, myself being at the top of the list, have a lower threshold of pain and suffering, both physical and emotional. We live in the land of plenty and have just about every creature comfort right at our fingertips, or pretty darn close. Personally speaking, despite the many challenges I've faced, I've been living a pretty charmed life. Looking back, I now realize that the lack of God in my life, combined with a good amount of professional and material success, left me ill-equipped to deal with painful situations when they came along.

The funny thing is, looking back on the many potholes along the way, every single problem or issue came with some sort of a silver lining. Without those challenges I wouldn't be where I am today. I am still hardly the type to immediately embrace suffering—as many of the great saints have done—when it comes my way. While I am strong in my faith, there is still a lot more whining than embracing going on. My faith, however, has taught me a thing or two about carrying our crosses. I have learned that if the Lord brings us to it, He is going to see us through it. I am also now in the habit of asking the Lord what He wants me to do with the suffering and what I am supposed to learn from it.

It's been said that it is not a matter of *if* we are going to suffer, but *when*. No one leaves this world unscathed. Embracing our troubles as opportunities rather than obstacles is a big part of the godly bucket list.

The issue of suffering is one of the toughest aspects of faith to grasp. All of us at some point have probably asked why a loving God would allow so much death, destruction, and misery? Whether it's 9-11, the Boston Marathon bombing, the shootings in Newtown and Aurora, or Superstorm Sandy, suffering just doesn't seem fair or to make much sense. But it wasn't supposed to be this way. Everything changed, as the Catechism explains, with the fall of man, or original sin:

> Man tempted by the devil, let his trust in his Creator die in his heart and, abusing his freedom, disobeyed God's command. This is what man's first sin consisted of. All subsequent sin would be disobedience toward God and lack of trust in goodness.
>
> In that sin man *preferred* himself to God and by that very act scorned him. He chose himself over and against God, against the requirements of his creaturely status and therefore against his own good. Constituted in holiness, man was destined to be fully "divinized" by God in glory. Seduced by the devil, he wanted to "be like God," but "without God, before God, and not in accordance with God." (CCC 397–398)

As the Church goes on to explain, the reverberations from the fall of man reach far and wide:

> The consequences of original sin and of all men's personal sins put the world as a whole in the sinful condition aptly described in St. John's expression "the sin of the world." This expression can also

refer to the negative influence exerted on people by communal situations and social structures that are the fruit of men's sins. (CCC 208)

Blessed John Paul II said, "Sin is never singular." The good and bad choices we make have a ripple effect on everyone and everything, including nature. Probably one of the best explanations of this effect came from Archbishop Thomas Wenski of Miami, who in a September 2005 column for the United States Conference of Catholic Bishops commented on the devastation of Hurricane Katrina:

> We live in a fallen and thus imperfect world. And oftentimes the forces of nature—earthquakes, tornadoes, and other natural disasters—can suggest that our planet itself is "in rebellion" against the original order of a loving Creator God. And that rebellion seen in nature—from the perspective of faith—can be said to mirror the rebellion of the human heart.

In his column, Archbishop Wenski makes a point of not blaming victims for the evils visited upon them. But we can't go around blaming God either. Think about the idea of having free will when making decisions. Human beings for a variety of reasons are behind the wars, industrialization, pollution, and environmental hazards that have had a major impact on the planet. It is possible to see how in some very practical ways, the choices made by us could have a negative impact and possibly affect the natural balance of the environment. But God never leaves us alone. As the archbishop stresses, we have a God who knows about immense suffering from firsthand experience:

> Jesus however does give us an insight on how God deals with the tragedies that afflict us. God does not remain remote or indifferent to the plight of his fallen creation. In Christ, the Word became Flesh. God became man. Rather than distancing Himself from people and their tragedies, He draws close to them. From the Cross, He stands in solidarity with all the pain experienced by us in our fallenness. Despair, destruction, death will not have the last word: rather the transformative power of his resurrection will define the human project anchored in hope.

And just as with everything else in our lives, to get a better understanding of suffering and what to do with it, we need to go to the cross. If Jesus, who is God, and nothing but pure love, was whipped, beaten, spat upon, mocked, and eventually nailed to a cross, why would we expect to go to our graves with barely a splinter? When we encounter suffering, we need to remember what Jesus did with that cross. What appeared to be the greatest defeat turned out to be salvation for the world. Suffering is our chance to turn our own crosses into crowns of glory. If this recipe reads too pie-in-the-sky, stop and reflect upon your own experience. Think about the times that have led to positive growth and change. Most likely, lessons learned did not follow the happiest times of your life. Most of the people I know grow when they've been challenged, made some bad choices on a personal or professional level, or were hurt in some way. Or, to quote an old Arab proverb: "All sunshine makes a desert."

In 1993, I was fired from a top TV position. Although it happened more than twenty years ago, the details—including the looks on the faces of my coworkers as I walked out the door with my box of notepads, pens, story files, and family photos—are still clear in my mind. Overnight, I went from covering the top stories on the evening news to standing in the unemployment line. Talk about the exalted being humbled. While it's difficult enough to lose a job, doing so in the public eye was exasperating. I couldn't go to the post office, the doctor's office, or the frozen yogurt shop down the street without someone asking why I'd disappeared from the airwaves. I always wear my heart on my sleeve, so the pain on my face was for all to see. With the exception of a little bit of freelance writing here and there, I was out of work. The Detroit area was going through yet another rough patch in the economy, and all major industries were impacted, including the news business. It was, as I often share in my testimony talks, my own time in the desert. I was known for being a hard-hitting reporter and the go-to gal when it came to breaking news. Weekends, nights, holidays didn't matter. If there was a story, I was on it. You snooze in the news biz, you lose. As I continued to walk through this desert licking my wounds, I wondered what I still believed. I felt I had sacrificed so much for my career and had just about lost my marriage in the process.

Little did I know, as Archbishop Wenski reminds us, that Jesus was walking beside me all the time and had already begun to provide the answer. As I've described earlier in this book, the answer came through a men's Bible study group that my husband had enrolled in the previous year. The Bible study had changed his life, and eventually it would change mine too. The Bible class led to Dominick's furthering his faith studies at Sacred Heart Major Seminary in Detroit. His rediscovering Christ and the Church gave him the strength, patience, and wisdom to deal with a very difficult wife.

It was about six months into my unemployment when I finally took some of my husband's sage advice. He had been encouraging me to get back to Mass and to ask God back into my life. So I gave it a shot and reached out to the God of my childhood, the God I first truly met when I received the sacrament of Holy Eucharist. I always knew God was real. After I left Catholic grade school, I just didn't pay much attention to God unless I really needed Him—and, boy, I needed Him so much during those days and months after being fired. So out of sheer frustration and desperation, and after one more day of unemployment and unanswered job inquiries, I stared at the crucifix hanging on the wall in our bedroom and asked Him to come back into my life. It wasn't a very sophisticated prayer. It was actually more like "Help Lord. SOS."

Within two weeks of saying that simple prayer, I received a call from another TV station in town, the top local network affiliate. Before I knew it, I was sitting in the station manager's office along with the news director discussing a new position as a general-assignment reporter. It was then I thought of my pretty much one-sided conversation with God and thought, *Hmmm, this Christian thing is pretty darn nice. You say a prayer, and the answer literally comes calling. I could get used to this.*

Finally I started to put the pieces of the suffering puzzle together. I realized that if I had remained part of the ten o'clock news team, I never would have reached out for God. It wasn't a work ethic that I had adopted, but a misguided obsession with all things career. There was no way God was going to get my attention in the midst of a bustling newsroom. I had to be yanked out of my comfort zone and dumped into the desert to wake up and smell the cappuccino. The six months away from the hectic schedule of a TV newsperson also allowed time for my husband and me to get back on track, including some marriage counseling and a Marriage Encounter retreat. Most important, we went back to Mass as a couple and started our way back home to the Catholic Church. These were the very first steps taken to turn our marriage around and to saying yes to a series of messes in my life. Over and over again, these steps eventually led me to "turn misery into ministry," as Joyce Meyer says. Although I didn't see it at the time, the turmoil at work and home would be most beneficial in the future. If I've learned anything at all in my years, it's that we never stop learning. And we can learn a lot from our mistakes to help other people along the way.

Many success stories come from the mess of

brokenness, or lots of Good Fridays. When I had the opportunity to interview Joyce Meyer many years ago, she discussed how she turned the misery of her own childhood sexual abuse into a worldwide Christian ministry. She speaks to millions of people on radio and TV every day and has written dozens of inspiring and motivating books. Meyer insisted she would not be nearly as effective as an evangelist without her painful past. Her wounds and afflictions, which have long been healed through her strong Christian faith, are key to her connection with her listeners, viewers, and readers. As a journalist, and for me personally, those people who turn what seems at first to be insurmountable tragedy into triumph are always my favorites to interview and write about.

When I think of those who have said yes to the mess and welcomed God's grace into their lives, a special ministry in suburban Detroit comes to mind. Paint a Miracle began after a successful pediatric dentist, Dale Propson, was hit by a drunk driver and suffered a massive brain injury, leaving his sight impaired. Dr. Propson went through years of rehab and therapy, and as the Propson family explained on my radio program, he tried a number of various hobbies, but he would usually end up disappointed in himself and more frustrated than when he began. That all changed when an aide decided to take him to an art studio. Dr. Propson at first didn't want to go inside. What was the point? How could anyone paint in his condition? The owner of the studio explained that art comes from the heart, not the eyes. So Dale Propson gave painting a shot and enjoyed it so much he encouraged his family to open their own studio to help others with disabilities. Dr. Propson turned the misery of his accident into ministry in 2002, when Paint a Miracle opened in Rochester, Michigan. The artists' drawings, paintings, and ceramics are exhibited and sold not only in the gallery, but around the suburban Detroit area. Most important, Paint a Miracle has raised awareness concerning people with disabilities. Dr. Propson feels like a contributing member of society again, and the gallery has brought immense joy and peace to his family, as well as strengthening their Catholic faith.

Another amazing beauty-into-ashes story centers on the annual Women Helping Women fashion show put on each May in the Detroit area by Grace Centers of Hope, a Christ-centered outreach serving the homeless and disadvantaged. Grace Centers runs shelters for both men and women, also servicing those who have been abused or are addicted to drugs and alcohol. The fashion show, now considered one of the top charity events in the Detroit area, all began with one woman who suffered greatly at the hands of an abusive husband. She was able to escape the domestic violence situation and was determined, once she had recovered, to do something to help other women finding themselves in the same painful circumstances. She came up with the idea of a fashion show featuring some of the female clients at Grace Centers' women's shelter. Since low self-esteem is such a major obstacle for domestic violence victims to overcome, why not help these women feel and look beautiful inside and out. The organizers chose a butterfly as their signature image for all their promotional materials, because they see the show, which raises hundreds of thousands of dollars each year for the women's shelter, as a way to help victims break out of their old cocoons and begin a new life. I have had the great privilege of serving as an emcee of this wonderful event. And there are few dry eyes in the house when the Grace Centers clients walk the runway.

In addition to these inspiring stories of adults making mature decisions to say yes to the mess, sometimes it's the youngest among us who surprise us with a strength and wisdom beyond their years. My pastor, Monsignor Michael Bugarin, confirms that sometimes it's the children who process and apply the concept of redemptive suffering more readily than adults. In an article for his parish bulletin, he referenced Jesus's words in Matthew 11:25:

At that time Jesus said in reply, "I give praise to you, Father, Lord of heaven and earth, for although you have hidden these things from the wise and the learned you have revealed them to the childlike."

Monsignor Bugarin went on to write:

I recall one of our teens saying it was better he had a terminal illness than either of his siblings. He knew God had given it to him for a reason. He would often visit other oncology pediatric patients while he himself was receiving chemotherapy. He wasn't focused on himself but looked for ways he could teach others through his illness. He turned his cross into something redemptive for himself and for those around him.

As Monsignor explained, the effort this young man made to step outside of his own pain helped him and the other patients realize they were not alone. In the famous Peace Prayer of Saint Francis, we are told among other things, that "it is in giving that we receive." The young cancer patient was greeted during his hospital "rounds" by plenty of warm smiles and thank-yous. By giving others encouragement, he received even more encouragement in return.

Not every tribulation we go through is going to

result in some sort of ministry. My theory is, however, that suffering should never go to waste. If nothing else, we can simply become better at making the most of some pretty unpleasant situations. Three of my favorite female saints—Saint Teresa of Ávila, Saint Catherine of Siena, and Saint Thérèse of Lisieux—are great role models for all Christians, and they can help us not only with such big issues as serious illness, relationship problems, or career crises, but with those everyday annoyances like traffic jams, minor aches and pains, and the coworkers, nasty neighbors, and other people in our life who drive us nuts.

At the age of seven, Saint Catherine of Siena dedicated her virginity to Christ. It's probably no surprise that women seven hundred years ago didn't have too many options. Marrying into a wealthy family was seen as a way to secure a young girl's future. So imagine the surprise and dismay of Catherine's parents when they learned that at such a young age, their daughter had made up her mind not to marry. They were stunned but believed she was going through a phase that would surely wear off and continued in their efforts to find their daughter a suitable husband. As the years went by, they kept pushing. Catherine, however, kept pushing right back.

Determined to make her point about already being bound in spiritual matrimony to God, and to make herself less attractive to the young Sienese suitors, Catherine cut off all her beautiful hair. Her mother was so upset that, to punish her, she made Catherine perform the tasks of a servant girl, certain that after a few days of cooking and cleaning for her huge family, which included two dozen siblings, Catherine would give in and agree to marry. Can you imagine what cooking and cleaning for a clan that size must have been like in fourteenth-century Italy? Given the hard labor involved, most would consider Catherine's situation quite a cross. Instead, Catherine truly said yes to the mess. When asked by a family friend, who also happened to be a priest, how she was handling the heavy workload, she said it was easy—she just pretended that her family was the Holy Family. She simply imagined her father as the Lord, her mother as the Blessed Mother, and her brothers as the apostles.

During the mid-sixteenth century, Saint Teresa of Ávila began her work to reform the Carmelite religious order, which was no easy task. Life in the first convent she entered was more like hanging out at the local Starbucks. She was encouraged to have lots of visitors, which led to her slipping into a worldly life, despite being part of a religious community. There was a lot more talking and gossiping than prayer. Eventually she realized that God was calling her to bring the order back to the basics. However, when word got around that she was going to press for a simple life of prayer and poverty, she was rejected by many in the Carmelite order and denounced by some Church leaders.

Saint Teresa, now considered one of the great Christian mystics, left behind a large volume of spiritual writing, including *The Way of Perfection*, *The Interior Castle*, and her own autobiography, *The Life of Teresa of Jesus*. But this same saint had a lighter and more joyful side. She had a dry sense of humor and was also known to be very direct with the Lord. On one occasion, during her struggles in reforming her order, she said out loud, "Lord if this is the way you treat your friends, no wonder you have so few." She loved to dance and to play the tambourine. Once, when she noticed some of her sisters were lacking joy in their devotions and prayer life, she exclaimed: "Lord preserve us from sour-faced saints." Amen!

Fast-forward about 320 years to the Carmelite convent in Lisieux, France, the home of another much-loved and great female saint, Saint Thérèse, "the Little Flower of Jesus." Thérèse was known for her "little way" of seeking holiness in the ordinary and the everyday. According to the Society of the Little Flower, a ministry that helps promote devotion to Saint Thérèse, the saint carried out this "little way" through a regular commitment to the tasks and to the people she met in her everyday life.

Thérèse had a hard time concentrating during the community prayer time, thanks to an older nun who had the habit of rattling her rosary beads and making other unpleasant noises. As Thérèse explained in her writings, what she really wanted to do was to stare the sister down right there in the chapel in hopes of getting her to stop making such a racket. Instead, the saint decided the noise was a gift meant for her purification, a "little opportunity of bearing with one of my sisters." She would later refer to the noise as "music." Talk about turning lemons into lemonade!

What I love about the saints is that, yes, they are saints—great holy women and men of God who have left behind volumes of teaching and great examples. But they are also human. They sinned. They made a lot of mistakes. They struggled. That's why the Church gives us the saints. If we took the time to get to know the saints a little bit better, we might learn some good lessons about life, especially about suffering. Brief glimpses into their lives and reflections on their actions may provide clues as to why God allows us to go through trials, as well as how to handle those trials. Try this one on for size: "God won't protect us from that which can perfect us." I can't remember where I heard that line, but it sums up the idea of "live in the mess" pretty nicely. God doesn't want us to suffer. He does allow some things to happen to us because they could lead, as they did in my life, to a major awakening and a much more rewarding life.

On the surface, suffering and happiness don't seem to belong in the same sentence. They appear to be polar opposites. Suffering is a synonym for pain and misery, so how does happiness come into play? We have to take a look at the bigger picture and not dwell on our temporary circumstances. We need to try and see how a negative experience can, for example, teach us a valuable lesson that will help us in the future. Christianity is not only honest enough to tell us the truth, but loving enough to give us *the truth,* as in the person of Jesus Christ, to help us deal with and grow from our pain.

> I have told you this so that you might have peace in me. In the world you will have trouble, but take courage, I have conquered the world. (John 16:33)

Years ago, after I came back to the Church, a Baptist minister and a dear friend of mine, Pastor Kent Clark, told me, "Teresa, God doesn't waste His time. Everything we go through can be used in some way, shape, or form for His greater glory." When Pastor

Clark shared those words, I happened to be at a crossroads in my career, wondering whether my years in the secular media added up to anything more than burnout. At the time, I was working in what would turn out to be my last hurrah in the news business as the news director at an FM radio station, a position I took after leaving television news. I didn't know where to go or where I fit in. Once I wound up back on local TV news, though, I thought I would finish my career like a lot of the other successful newspeople who had gone before me. I was planning to ride off into the TV news sunset doing a live report from the inner city or saying "So long, Motown" from behind the anchor desk. I wasn't prepared for anything other than the scenario I had painted for myself. After all, the TV news position seemed to have come in the form of a direct answer to prayer. I wasn't ready for the ugly changes taking place in the news business. Of course, I had no inkling of the incredible journey on which I was about to embark. Pastor Clark also left me with an important verse for anyone trying to make their way through a rough spot. It's from Saint Paul's Epistle to the Romans:

> We know that all things work for good for those who love God, who are called according to His purpose. (Romans 8:28)

As crazy as it seems, suffering serves us well in the category of God's bucket list for happiness. When Jesus took the apostles to the region of Caesarea Philippi, He explained that anyone who follows Him will have to take up their cross, and then some:

> For whoever wishes to save his life will lose it, but whoever loses his life for my sake and that of the Gospel will save it. What profit is there for one to gain the whole world and forfeit his life? (Mark 8:35–36)

At first glance, it does seem quite scary. Losing our life? Seriously? Yes, when it comes to losing our life by giving up our own agendas in exchange for something so much better—God's plan for our life. Looking back on my own tug-of-war with God, I knew deep down I was miserable. Things weren't going quite as smoothly as I thought they should. I had grandiose plans after returning to the Catholic Church of being a Christian light within the secular newsroom. It was nice while it lasted, but it didn't last long. Still, I didn't want to give up on that idea. As I was explaining to my friend Pastor Clark, I believed I was being called to do just that, so why would God want that to change? And why was I hanging on so tightly?

Perhaps I knew things were going to be different, and that once again I had to die to myself and to some of the old dreams I was clinging to. Part of me was convinced that most of my suffering on the professional level was over. I was also not sure I could do anything else, since reporting was the only type of work I had ever known. But once I "let go and let God," as I had in the prayer I had said out loud in my bedroom a few years earlier, God took that next yes and slowly moved me into a new and incredible life as a media evangelist. And guess what? I am still using my gift of gab, telling stories, and reporting the news. However, now I am confident that I am reporting the best possible news there is: the saving message of the Gospel.

In 1984, Blessed Pope John Paul II gave the world a great gift through his apostolic letter *Salvifici Doloris* ("On the Redemptive Suffering of Christ"). This document was issued long before the pope would be diagnosed with debilitating Parkinson's disease. The illness would lead him, and those who cared to follow his arduous journey, into a much more profound understanding of what we've been discussing all along: what Catholic theology refers to as redemptive suffering. John Paul could have easily been considered an expert on the topic. By the time he was twenty, he had lost all the members of his immediate family, including his parents and his older brother. Growing up in Poland, he had witnessed the horrors of the Nazi regime. In 1981, only three years after he had begun his pontificate, he was seriously injured in an assassination attempt on his life in Saint Peter's Square. How, then, given the tragedies he had both seen and personally experienced, was John Paul II able to be so joyful? He was considered one of the most influential leaders of the twentieth century. Millions, and not just Catholics, regularly flocked to his events as he traveled around the world spreading the Gospel. His funeral on April 8, 2005, saw the largest gathering of heads of state in history—with, according to a variety of sources, four kings; five queens; at least seventy presidents and prime ministers; and more than fourteen leaders of other religions. How could someone who had encountered persecution, pain, and evil in such a variety of forms continually tell Christians to "be not afraid"?

In *Salvici Doloris* 26, John Paul says:

Christ does not explain in the abstract the reasons for suffering, but before all else he says: "Follow me!" Come! Take part through your suffering in this work of saving the world, a salvation achieved through my suffering! Through my Cross. Gradually, *as the individual takes up his cross*, spiritually uniting himself to the Cross of Christ, the salvific meaning of suffering is revealed before him. He does not discover this meaning at his own human level, but at the level of the suffering of Christ. At the same time, however, from this level of Christ the salvific meaning of suffering *descends to man's level* and becomes, in a sense, the individual's personal response. It is then that man finds in his suffering interior peace and even spiritual joy.

None of us wants to suffer. However, since suffering is inevitable, isn't it much better to learn how best to face it and to become a better and more fulfilled person because of it? What I have trained myself to do in the midst of any sort of mess is to use the experience as a sort of holy exercise, a means to get me into better spiritual shape. *Okay, Lord, what am I supposed to be taking away from this latest life quiz, and how might I apply it in other areas?* Oh, yes, I squirm a lot and not just at first. I mean, seriously, who am I kidding? I am certainly never going to be under the Catholic big top with the likes of Saint Teresa, Saint Catherine, and Saint Thérèse. But when I stop and really think about my latest test, I also smile, wondering what the Lord has up His sleeve and what He is going to do with yet another one of my messes. I smile because I know from firsthand experience that

He never disappoints. As Saint Paul wrote in 1 Thessalonians 5:16–18:

> Rejoice always. Pray wihout ceasing. In all circumstances give thanks, for this is the will of God for you in Christ Jesus.

5.

Live with Understanding

Men occasionally stumble over the truth,
but most of them pick themselves up and
hurry off as if nothing had happened.
—Winston Churchill

It was another one of those "aha" moments. I was preparing for my radio show and came across an interesting story regarding yet another rise in the number of cases of sexually transmitted infections. The statistics released in February of 2013 from the Centers for Disease Control (CDC) showed that there were about 20 million new infections each year in the United States, with half of all young people ages fifteen to twenty-four shouldering a substantial burden of these infections.

The story seemed like a tap on the shoulder from God pointing out to the world where our oversexualized culture is leading us. And it's not a very happy place, even though the messages on TV programs, in music videos, and in one film after the next fail to show the negative side of sexual promiscuity.

It was also a reminder of the need to be better educated.

God does give us free will, but He also gives us plenty of evidence that His way is *the* high way—or the highest way—if only we would start paying attention. We seem to be able to do our homework and get educated on plenty of other topics: choosing the right college, planning our finances, buying or selling a home, taking that special vacation. But when it comes to those below-the-belt issues and other subjects dealing with morality, we seem to "hurry off," as Churchill said, and ignore the truth placed before us.

In 1 Thessalonians 5:20, Saint Paul tells us to "test everything, hold on to every good and reject every kind of evil." As a talk show host and Catholic speaker, I'm always looking for ways to bring the truth of God's Word and Catholic teaching to my audience in a practical way. As much as I love sharing the beauty and depth of my faith, witnessing doesn't always have to include quotes from the Catechism or the Bible. Studies such as the report from the CDC, a secular entity with no religious dog in the fight, are an effective way to "test everything" and to help those struggling with their faith to see the truth in God's laws. It helps them to see that His ways are not backward or oppressive but instead give us the best chance for real freedom and happiness.

God is the great scientist. Truth is truth, but what exactly is truth? How do we answer this age-old question that Pilate asked Jesus? Christians know the answer: Truth is a person, as Pope Emeritus Benedict XVI told seminarians at Saint Joseph's Seminary in Yonkers, New York, during his 2008 visit to the United States. And that person is Jesus Christ.

> Dear friends, truth is not an imposition. Nor is it simply a set of rules. It is a discovery of the One who never fails us; the One whom we can always trust. In seeking truth we come to live by belief because ultimately truth is a person: Jesus Christ.

It was the search for the truth in my life that led me back to the person of Jesus Christ and the Catholic Church. It's interesting that when that journey began, the search was centered on finding meaning, purpose, and joy again in my own life. However, my commitment to my faith would also force me to reevaluate a lot more than my work as a journalist. Jesus was about to rock my world—or more precisely my worldview—big-time. My love for Him and my ability to research and report the facts would eventually force me to connect the dots between what was happening in our culture and the truth of the Bible and the Church teachings.

Scripture tells us in Hebrews 13:8 that "Jesus is the same yesterday and today and forever." We can say the same thing about truth—no matter how we try to suppress, deny, or twist it to fit our lives, it never changes. As Archbishop Fulton J. Sheen is often credited with saying: "The truth is still the truth even if nobody believes it, and a lie is still a lie even if everyone believes it."

I didn't practice my faith for many years. But my life is a perfect example of how God is still out there trying to speak to us. He can and does use all means to get our attention—in my case, even a quote in a trade magazine. The quote I'm talking about was a profound one from an address John Paul gave to journalists at the United Nations at the end of his first visit to the United States as pope in 1979. I came across it in a trade magazine published by the Society of Professional Journalists years before my journey back to the Church. And it was all about truth:

> You are indeed servants of the truth; you are its tireless transmitters, diffusers, defenders. You are dedicated communicators, promoting unity among all nations by sharing truth among all peoples.
>
> If your reporting does not always command the attention you would desire of it, if it does not always conclude with the success that you would wish, do

not grow discouraged. Be faithful to the truth and to its transmission, for truth endures; truth will not go away. Truth will not pass or change.

Few of us in college journalism programs during the late '70s and '80s had any idea that our craft would become a slave to ratings and particular agendas, leaving the truth, for the most part, on the editing-room floor. We were starry-eyed and idealistic. We were all going to be the next Woodward or Bernstein. The quote from John Paul II came promptly out of the magazine and into a frame I carried from the college dorms and then from one newsroom to the next. It sits in the very same frame, a little worse for wear, in my home office and studio today, although now it carries much more meaning.

I began my news career in 1981. By then the women's movement had made its mark on me and plenty of other young female college graduates. Guilty as charged. I swallowed much of the feminist ideology hook, line, and sinker. You'd think this radical feminist would have gotten a clue that God was going to shake things up a bit when my future husband came into my life exactly one week after college graduation. But some of us are a little slower than others. Six months later we were engaged, and two years later we were indeed walking down the aisle. We were going along merrily and didn't think much about our use of birth control. We knew somewhere in the back of our minds what the Catholic Church taught about it, but since it was hardly mentioned during our marriage prep courses, we made excuses to ourselves. If the Church wasn't all that worried about it, why should we be so concerned? Years later, after our long road back to the Church, my husband revealed to me that he had always felt uncomfortable with our nonconformity to Church teaching. We realized now it was the Holy Spirit speaking to his heart.

Every once in a while, truth would stick its annoying little head into the middle of my perfect little world. As a married couple we could talk about anything except abortion. Having bought into the lies of feminism, I was staunchly pro-choice. To my husband, the engineer with his extensive background in math and science, life began at conception. It was a child, not a choice, and a no-brainer to my husband. "It's biology 101," he would tell me. My response was based on little more than pride, emotion, and cultural conditioning from four years on a liberal college campus, and, most important, the absence of God in my life.

"It's a woman's body, and how she uses it should be her choice and up to no one else."

If you had asked me to explain the Church teaching on abortion, you would have received a very long, blank stare as your answer. I knew the Church was against abortion, but I couldn't tell you why, except that it might have something to do with that "Thou shall not kill" item mentioned by Moses in the Ten Commandments. Unfortunately, most of the abortion supporters I have interviewed and have known over the years were, like me, acting on emotion, misinformation, conditioning, and their own refusal to take a closer look at what abortion really is and what it does—and not only to the vulnerable child in the womb. Despite the countless resources out there, in many cases we are just not connecting the dots. The Kaiser Family Foundation study I mentioned earlier in the book reported that Americans are consuming all types of information from the media at a rate of five to six hours a day. But if they are not listening to Catholic or evangelical media, it's highly doubtful they will have heard much at all about abortion, at least when it comes to its negative consequences.

A few years ago, while giving a presentation to Catholic grade school students about the importance of making wise choices even at their young age, I tried my best to drive home the point that choices can have long-term consequences. They got the whole concept of discipline. They understood that the guidelines we and their parents were giving them were for their benefit and not for their harm. Most moms and dads were giving them a structure to protect them and help them take healthy, rather than harmful, steps. As a result, they knew they were loved, cared for, and safe. But so many of us who understand the need to provide discipline and structure for children somehow can't look at God the same way, as a loving, caring parent who wants the best for His children.

One way to think about the structure God gives us in the Commandments and Church teaching is to think of it as a day at the beach. If you're a beach bum like me, you may love the water, but you probably don't relish the idea of going out into one of Michigan's powerful Great Lakes or the Atlantic Ocean by yourself, even if you're a very good swimmer. Anyone with any experience around the water knows conditions can change in an instant, and that, even if they're a good swimmer, they're no match for the waves or undercurrents. Isn't it much more relaxing when we know there's a lifeguard looking on and when the swimming area is well-marked by buoys and safety ropes? Trying to get through life without God's guidance reminds me of those signs you sometimes see along abandoned shorelines: NO LIFEGUARD ON DUTY. SWIM AT YOUR OWN RISK. But it seems the world is telling us, through the culture, "Come on in. The water is just fine." There is no mention of the undercurrents, the jellyfish, or the great white sharks. We're making major decisions, based not only on bad information, but, in many cases, on no information at all.

My own struggles, personally and professionally, were based in part on a lack of accurate information. My opinions regarding moral issues such as birth control and abortion, as well as my decisions to put my career first above everything and everyone else in my life, were again based on a lack of accurate information, combined with messages from a radical feminist agenda. The National Organization for Women and other feminist groups gaining prominence in the '70s and '80s convinced us that the "my way or the highway" would guarantee our road to fulfillment. And yet, in reality, my world was slowly falling apart.

I think Pope Emeritus Benedict would agree with my beach analogy. During one of his weekly Angelus messages on September 2, 2012, he told pilgrims that God's law brings personal liberation.

God's law is His Word, which guides man on the path of life, releases him from the slavery of selfishness and introduces him to the land of true freedom and life. For this reason in the Bible the Law is not seen as a burden, an overwhelming limitation, but as the Lord's most precious gift, the testimony of his fatherly love, of His desire to be close to His people, to be their ally and write His people a love story.

That's what happens when we, as Churchill said, stumble into the truth but then run the other way. By not connecting the dots, we are wading into dangerous territory and turning ourselves into shark bait.

God started to slowly chip away at my hardened heart on the abortion issue during a campaign in my home state of Michigan to end welfare-funded abortion. My radio news director asked me to do a thirty-minute public-affairs show featuring both sides in the abortion debate. One representative from Right to Life–Lifespan and one representative from NARAL (the National Abortion and Reproductive Rights League, now referred to as NARAL–Pro Choice America) were brought into the studio for the taping.

What happened over the course of the interview would eventually be life changing for me because of the very well-documented medical information shared by the pro-life representative as compared with the lack of information and the highly emotional responses of the NARAL spokeswoman. There was a little voice inside my head repeating "Say it isn't so."

The Right to Life–Lifespan representative, in addition to volunteering in the pro-life movement, was a registered nurse. She began to outline not just the obvious problems for the baby in the womb, but also the medical and psychological complications for the woman. If it were all about choice, why, as this passionate nurse explained, were surveys showing one too many women being pressured into an abortion? Why weren't these women told there was help available through pregnancy resource centers and other sources if they decided to keep their baby? Why didn't abortion clinics screen for coercion or discuss adoption?

Something else struck me about the two guests sitting in the radio studio that day. The pro-life person was passionate and at the same time extremely peaceful. The NARAL representative was angry almost to the point of erupting right there on the spot. She said nothing about the child and only kept going back to choice, choice, choice, which sounded a lot more like me, myself, and I. She had virtually no comeback to the lack of information given to the women showing up at the doors of her abortion clinic, nor about the choices of the baby and the others that would be affected by an abortion. The woman "choosing" an abortion eliminates the "choice" of the baby whose life is being terminated, as well as that of the man who fathered that child, who may want to choose differently.

That fateful interview planted a seed, but one that wouldn't sprout for quite some time. Eventually that interview would come back to me and, combined with my reversion, forced me to finally do what someone who called herself a Catholic and worked as a reporter should have done in the first place: get educated. Do the homework and read what the Church and pro-life groups actually have to say about the issue. Maybe the Church wasn't just some archaic and out-of-touch institution. Maybe these organizations weren't just a bunch of religious zealots. Maybe there was a bigger issue here. Could it be that the Church and the pro-life movement did have the best interests of both the baby and the mother in mind? The answer to that question is, of course, a big yes. Gradually the truth was able to break through to me.

Reading papal encyclicals, including Pope Paul VI's *Humanae Vitae* ("Of Human Life") and John Paul II's *Evangelium Vitae* ("Gospel of Life"), was the game changer for me. You didn't have to be a Nobel Prize winner, a rocket scientist, or a moral theologian to figure this one out. Some of the research from groups such as the Elliot Institute, a leader in the effort to break the silence concerning women and abortion, also forced me to take another look at this issue.

Among the institute's recent findings:

- 79 percent of women weren't told about available resources.
- 67 percent of women received no counseling before an abortion.
- 64 percent of women reported feeling pressured to have an abortion.
- The clinics involved failed to screen for coercion.
- Most women felt uncertain or rushed into the decision.

Not only were women being denied crucial information about the procedure of abortion, the same problem was occurring in regard to artificial contraception. And another can of worms was beginning to cause me many a sleepless night: my beloved profession was part of the misinformation machine! Studies showing an increased risk of breast cancer among women who had abortions were not being reported. Nor were the studies showing a laundry list of medical problems resulting from use of the birth control pill, even though the pill had long been considered a carcinogen and, like abortion, was connected strongly to an increased breast cancer risk. (The World Health Organization would in 2005 declare the birth control pill a Group 1 carcinogen.)

My industry was also ignoring the shoddy conditions at abortion facilities. The pro-abortion groups hid behind very convincing spin language. Besides their focus on "choice," they often said abortion rights were all about "reproductive rights" or "women's health." Any one person or group who tried to expose regular violations of health standards and medical complications with abortion and birth control were labeled as "antichoice" and "antiwoman" by the Planned Parenthoods and NARALs of the world, as well as the media, not to mention the numerous politicians who were right there ready to carry their version of the truth to the American public.

One of the most blatant examples of not dancing around the truth but denying it altogether happened in my home state of Michigan in the late spring of 2012. A package of bills was drafted and passed by the Michigan pro-life legislature, designed to hold the abortion industry to the same health and safety standards as other medical procedures. Now you would think that those who claim they are about all "reproductive health" or "women's health" would welcome measures to help ensure a woman's safety when seeking an abortion. Earlier in the year, Right to Life of Michigan had issued a shocking report titled "Abortion Abuses and State Regulatory Failure" regarding conditions at Michigan's thirty abortion facilities. Among the findings:

- Some abortion clinics in the state have operated for decades but have never been inspected.
- In Michigan, only four of the thirty surgical abortion operations are licensed and inspected.
- In numerous cases, abortion clinics were involved in the illegal dumping of fetal remains, patient records, and biohazard waste.
- Clinics routinely have insufficient recovery wards that lack basic monitoring and resuscitation equipment.
- Many Michigan abortion operations have refused timely transport of patients to a hospital during emergency situations.

The legislation would also outlaw doctors prescribing the abortion drug RU-486 over the Internet. Abortion doctors would never actually physically see or examine the women but would merely "consult" them over a webcam.

Pro-choice politicians, backed by the pro-abortion lobby, used the proposed legislation as an opportunity to break out into song and dance—almost literally—not only inside the state capitol building during legislative hearings, but outside on the state capitol steps as well. The drama queens cried out and went so far as to welcome Eve Ensler, the author of the controversial *Vagina Monologues* play, to Michigan to take part in a major protest. There was a lot of chanting and ranting going on, complete with a giant V made out of cloth and strewn across the capitol steps. Ensler even performed her play as a statement of support for the lawmakers who claimed they were silenced during debate because of their opposition to the legislation. Actually, it was their long-winded testimony, filled with vulgar language and accusations of rape against those backing the proposed laws, that put an end to their commentary—which was all smoke and mirrors and nothing about the truth. No connecting the dots here, since the dots, as in the dangers facing abortion-minded women across Michigan, barely saw the light of day in the public forum. Unless someone was listening to Christian or conservative talk radio, they wouldn't have heard a peep about the jaw-dropping report that included evidence from police agencies, medical officials, and the Michigan attorney general. The public was being had, and they didn't even know it.

As I slowly and painfully discovered, these regular

song-and-dance routines had been going on for decades, beginning with the sexual revolution and the so-called women's liberation movement. And I had swallowed much of the propaganda.

While we were making a lot of advances on Wall Street and Madison Avenue, the reality of the situation was in many ways taking women backward, not moving them forward. It's not that women didn't deserve equal pay and equal opportunity. Even the Church acknowledged the mistreatment of women by corporate America and by governmental policies in the United States and elsewhere. It's just that women were told that, for the most part, they had to deny their natural inclinations in order to get ahead. We were also led to believe that the "I am woman, hear me roar" battle cry made famous in 1972 by Helen Reddy's hit single by the same name, was all about being respected for our IQs instead of our bra size. We wanted to be treated as equals. Why should women be denied in the boardroom or the bedroom for that matter? If men could have the corner office and hop from bed to bed without any ramifications, why should they be the only ones having all the fun?

Somewhere along the path to fulfillment we were brainwashed into thinking that making bold moves in the boardroom and the bedroom would make us be seen less as objects and more as men's equals. Who were we kidding? While some of the changes in education, career advancement, and the like resulting from the women's movement are to be greatly applauded, the feminists lost their way and took a lot of us into a land of confusion. We ended up not with less bondage, but more. Some fifty-plus years later, *Fifty Shades of Grey* is considered practically required reading for today's modern woman. We are now more objectified than ever before. Did the bra burners of the '60s really want their daughters and granddaughters to believe that being bound up and called a man's *submissive*, like the lead female character in *Fifty Shades of Grey*, is the ideal existence?

The teachings of Scripture and the Church don't depend on us. They aren't true because we believe them. People of faith believe and practice these teachings because *they are true*. Once we open our eyes, we don't have to look very far at all to see the proof of God's plan being the better plan for our lives. Interestingly enough, most of the evidence backing these teachings is coming from secular sources. In 2007, the American Psychological Association produced a groundbreaking report concerning the oversexualization of girls. Ironically, or maybe not so ironically, this report sounded a lot like what Pope Paul VI had to say in *Humanae Vitae*, written almost forty years earlier. Of course, the APA report wasn't looking at contraception and abortion. It was looking at what happens to a girl when she believes she is valued only for her physical and sexual attractiveness. The report stated that oversexualization can lead to a number of problems, including eating disorders, depression, and low self-esteem, and that the media were to blame in a big way for oversexualizing girls. Media icons such as Victoria's Secret, Bratz Dolls, and Britney Spears were named among the culprits.

In July 2012, researchers at Knox College in Illinois released a study involving elementary school girls in the Midwest that showed that girls as young as six years old are beginning to think of themselves as sex objects. The researchers used paper dolls to assess self-sexualization. One doll was decked out in a miniskirt and a tight midriff top that revealed skin, including cleavage. The other doll was dressed in attractive but modest clothes. When shown the two dolls, about 70 percent of the girls said they looked more like the sexy doll and that the sexy doll was more popular. It doesn't take a giant leap in thought to see prophecy in the words of Pope Paul VI. He predicted more than four decades ago in *Humanae Vitae* that abortion and contraception, which put impure attention on human sexuality, would lead to the disrespect and objectification of women:

Another effect that gives cause for alarm is that a man who grows accustomed to the use of contraceptive methods may forget the reverence due to a woman, and disregarding her physical and emotional equilibrium, reduce her to being a mere instrument for the satisfaction of his own desires, no longer considering her as his partner whom he should surround with care and affection.

Although *Humanae Vitae* was released in 1968, in the twenty-first century it has proved terribly prescient. If we pay attention and if we ask God to reveal Himself to us, we will see the truth of God's Word and Church teaching being played out in real life. So it would also follow that taking the natural order of things seriously would be to our benefit.

Case in point: let's take another look at the natural law, or God's law as given to Moses in the Ten Commandments. Did you know that telling the truth as outlined in the commandment concerning not bearing false witness is actually linked to better health? So telling the truth and avoiding those little and not-so-little lies is really good for us. According to a "Science of Honesty" study presented at the American Psychological Association's annual convention in August 2012, honesty can significantly improve a person's mental and physical health:

"Recent evidence indicates that Americans average about 11 lies a week. We wanted to find out if living more honestly can actually cause better health. We found that the participants could purposefully and dramatically reduce their everyday lies and that it in turn was associated with significantly improved health," said Dr. Anita Kelly, lead author of the study and professor of pyschology at Notre Dame University.

Kelly and her coauthor conducted the experiment in honesty over ten weeks with 110 people ranging in age from 18 to 71 years old: 34 percent were adults, and 66 percent were college students. About half were asked to stop telling major and minor lies for the ten-week study period. The other half served as a control group and received no special instructions. Both groups came together weekly to complete health and relationship measures and to take a lie-detector test assessing the number of major and minor lies they had told that week. The study found the connection between lying less and improved health to be much stronger in the no-lie group. They experienced fewer health complaints such as headaches, sore throats, and tension and also reported improved social interactions.

The idea of doing unto others as you would have it done unto you, loving your neighbor as yourself—aka "the golden rule"—is not specifically found in the Ten Commandments, but there are various references to this idea in both the Old and New Testaments, including the Gospels. The message most commonly associated with Jesus is, of course, the idea of helping your neighbor. Here again, secular studies find that this biblically rooted principle of putting others first and doing good is also good for the body and soul.

Take volunteering, for example. In a review of recent research published by the Corporation for National and Community Service in 2007 and titled *The Health Benefits of Volunteering*, researchers found a significant connection between volunteering and good health: volunteers reported greater longevity, lower rates of depression, higher functional ability, and fewer incidences of heart disease. People usually volunteer to give to others, but they also receive much in return. They come away with a sense of purpose and are less likely to become fixated on their own troubles. Or, as Saint Francis of Assisi said in his much loved and much repeated words known as "The Peace Prayer of Saint Francis": "It is in giving that we receive."

You can see how Jesus did indeed rock my world and my worldview. The change didn't come easily. I had to work at it and get educated. That's true for all of us. The more we learn, the more we are able to make well-informed decisions. First, I had to take the information and try to put it into practice. Soon I could see how my life at home had changed for the better when my husband and I made God the center of our lives. Second, it was becoming easier to see what happens in the world when it leaves God behind. Last but not least, as someone who from her early days in journalism school believed the media were all about truth, I had to reconcile the fact that the news business had in many ways turned into just that—a business—and for the most part had lost its soul for the sake of profit and certain political ideologies. Repeatedly my eyes would wander back to the quote on my desk from John Paul II's address to journalists at the United Nations:

> Be faithful to the truth and to its transmission, for truth endures; truth will not go away. Truth will not pass or change.
>
> And I say to you—take it as my parting word to you—that the service of truth, the service of humanity through the medium of truth—is something worthy of your best years, your finest talents, your most dedicated efforts.

When I walked out of the secular newsroom for the last time, I knew the "service of the truth" was still my goal. Only now I would be serving the truth by helping others roll up their sleeves, do their homework, and get some badly needed education. If I could help just one person avoid the mistakes that I made, the effort would be worth it.

6.

Live by Confession

 We know what we are but not what we may become.
—William Shakespeare

I heard a retreat leader say several years ago: "God loves you right where you're at, but He also loves you too much to keep you there." This is another way of saying that God doesn't want us to spin our wheels or get stuck in a rut. So every now and then we're going to need a good spiritual push into the repair shop as we travel the road to the abundant life. It's important to take an occasional good look under the hood—to do some self-reflection and take stock of where we've been, where we are, and what we need to do to keep moving in the right direction. As the poet Carl Sandburg wrote in a letter to a friend:

> It is necessary now and then for a man to go away by himself and experience loneliness; to sit on a rock in the forest and to ask of himself, "Who am I, and where have I been, and where am I going?" . . . If one is not careful, one allows diversions to take up one's time—the stuff of life.

That sounds in some ways very calming and tranquil. But what it should also be, according to Saint Augustine, is challenging, because it's too easy to sit on that rock and get sidetracked into contemplating everything but ourselves:

> People travel to wonder at the height of the mountains, at the huge waves of the sea; at the long courses of rivers, at the vast compass of the ocean, at the circular motion of the starts; and they pass by themselves without wondering.

Tolstoy said that everyone thinks of changing the world, but no one thinks of changing themselves. How true. Take it from me. It's not always easy to take a good look at ourselves or to take stock. It can be frustrating, even painful. Maybe we are not where we want to be in life. Maybe we know, as in my case, that we have to come to terms with our faults and failings. I would like to say that I got into the habit of regularly taking stock on my own. However, it was actually the unpleasant circumstances surrounding a painful job loss that forced me to look in the mirror. I had a lot of time on my hands. If I could go back and do some things differently, I would have brought God into the taking-stock process a lot sooner. After all, He knows us better than we know ourselves. He created us in His image and likeness, and, as it says in Matthew 10:30: "Even the very hairs of your head have been counted." Most important, we need to find out where we are in our relationship with Him if the end goal is to find and fulfill His bucket list for happiness.

I'm a big fan of the Ten Commandments. They provide a good guide for self-examination: they can show us where we're being honest with ourselves and where we could use some fine-tuning. Okay, so maybe most of us haven't committed heinous mortal sins, but maybe you've neglected to pay some bills or have played a few numbers games with your taxes. Maybe you've told a few lies, or you've become so preoccupied with the welfare of your family that you've ignored a neighbor who might need help. Sin clogs our motors and can really slow us down.

One of the best tools to pack for our journey of self-examination is readily available in any local Catholic parish, and it costs a lot less than some glitzy seminar. It is free, and the benefits are eternal. It's the sacrament of Reconciliation, more commonly referred to as Confession. If you're trying to embrace God's bucket list, who better to talk to than God Himself? Okay, granted, you're talking to a priest during Confession, but God is present in the sacrament through what is known as *in persona Christi*, "in the person of Christ." Jesus is working through that priest who's helping you take a good look at yourself. Catholics are required to receive this sacrament at least once a year. Many spiritual directors suggest once a month to keep the spiritual parts running smoothly. Saint Francis de Sales said Confession can put the wind of grace back in our sails:

> In confession you not only receive absolution from the sins you confess, but also great strength to avoid them in the future, light to see them clearly, and abundant grace to repair whatever damage you have incurred.

Confession is the ultimate course in self-examination, and, as I said before, it doesn't cost anything except maybe an offering of humble pie. I guess you can say Confession is the repair shop for the soul. In between Confessions, an examination of conscience keeps the mystical motors running. Another way to look at it is that each sin is a little bit like a tiny fat deposit that clogs our arteries. Eventually, all the buildup can create a dangerous blockage that takes away our life.

As children of God, we are called to be saints. Nick Synko, who I mentioned earlier in the book, uses the acronym *S.A.I.N.T.* to help participants in his faith-based career-coaching workshops get started on the self-discovery path. He asks them to begin by taping several sheets of flip chart paper on a wall in their home. Then he says:

"On those flip chart pages, title the sheets: Skills? Abilities? Interests? Natural for me? Talents? Then begin filling the pages with those thoughts that you and others believe are your inventory of Skills, Abilities you possess, and so on. Of course pray and ask the Holy Spirit to work with you as you complete them.

The S.A.I.N.T. process, or something similar to it, can serve as another form of an examination of conscience. It's quite helpful and encouraging and gets the creative juices flowing when you sit down and actually take stock of what you have to offer God and the world.

In my case, I used a simple notepad to jot down my interests and also my concerns regarding the culture and the media climate. My own self-reflection helped me see that there were a lot of ideas, as well as frustrations, building up inside of me. What really bugged me, and what could I do about those nasty bugs? What miseries could translate into ministries and maybe even a little income? Mainly I was interested in positively affecting the media, as well as helping concerned citizens learn how to use the media wisely. So naturally, the thought of media awareness presentations in schools, parishes, and other venues came to mind. I did the self-inventory/taking-stock exercise more than once. The more I went back to that pad and paper and the more I asked for God's guidance, the more the ideas flowed and the more the frustrations subsided. I felt as if I could once again make a difference.

Another one of my big pet peeves as a reporter concerned the area of public relations. I saw a lot of PR firms taking advantage of companies and individuals. How PR clients were being misled was very evident at press conferences, where businesses and speakers came complete with virtual dog-and-pony shows because their PR firm had convinced them they had to spend a ton of money on slick press kits and glossy signs. Little did they know that, except for the basic information, those press kits ended up in the garbage. The signs were pretty much ignored by the cameras, since news stations were not looking to offer free advertising during a news story.

In addition to the often ridiculous and unnecessary formal press conferences, PR types would often demand to be put on monthly retainers but rarely came through with the media coverage that had been promised in exchange for their hefty fees. It was also pitiful to watch how poorly some performed behind the podium. It was obvious on several occasions that the PR firm had spent little or no time coaching its client. The client was not ready for prime time and had no business answering questions. I often said to myself while covering yet one more boring press conference, *If I ever own my own company, I will show people how to get news coverage without all the bells, whistles, and big budgets; and I will prepare them for the spotlight.*

Those thoughts ran through my mind as I was taking stock of my abilities, skills, and interests. I realized that incorporating media relations into my company services could be a very beneficial part of my business. As a reporter, I knew how to get a story covered. I had also given a lot of free advice over the years and joyfully watched several businesses do well by my suggestions. So I decided that public relations and media consulting would be one of the services I would offer through my company. Helping good corporate citizens get decent media coverage at a fair price was fulfilling a true public service.

Within media consulting, I made sure I offered seminars on crisis communications. It was another one of those "aha" moments for me during my inventory sessions. There had been one too many breaking news stories that involved dealing with one too many spokespersons. Usually these spokespersons were not speaking the same language even though they were representing the same operation. The left hand had no idea what the right hand was doing. In the meantime, all heck was breaking loose, and way too much confusing and conflicting information was going out over the airwaves. The same thought that would pop into my head during the dog-and-pony shows would pop into my head as I was covering a school shooting or a chemical spill: *If I ever own my own company, crisis communications training is going to be a big part of it.* "Managing the Media in a Crisis Situation" continues to be a vital seminar that I am asked to give in a variety of venues today.

So there I was, only out of the news business for a little over a month. I had formed my LLC, Teresa Tomeo Communications, and I already had two decent clients. One of my biggest desires was to get out there as a motivational speaker so I could really start addressing media-awareness issues. I had done some short talks, and some Knights of Columbus councils invited me to speak, as did friends who were in the local Rotary Club. I was getting frustrated with this area, though, and realized that one of the drawbacks of leaving radio was the loss of visibility. While I had a website, the Internet was not nearly as prominent as it is today. Boy, wouldn't it be great if I could get some media exposure somehow? I had no desire to be a newsperson again. I just needed an outlet.

Well, as Jesus says in Matthew 7:7: "Ask and you shall receive." Out of the blue, or so it seemed, I received a call from a friend of mine at the local evangelical station. They were looking for someone to take on a midday talk show. They couldn't offer me much in pay, but it would put me on the air for an hour a day on an FM powerhouse station with a huge Christian audience. A talk show was something new for me. Although I had been on the air for years and my mother says I came out of the womb talking, up until now my air time, outside of anchoring the news on occasion, was limited to two or three minutes. Now I was being handed a full hour.

I jumped at the challenge and ended up hosting *Christian Talk with Teresa Tomeo* for two years. The show consisted of interviews with leading Christian teachers and authors, as well as my own commentary. Many of the listeners remembered me from my secular TV and radio days. Soon requests for speaking engagements starting coming in. There was a special interest in my journey from secular media into the area of ministry. So little by little I began giving my testimony, and the motivational speaker in me was born.

Fellow author and Catholic evangelist Gary Zimak, from Following the Truth ministries, (www .followingthetruth.com) will tell you that taking stock means taking notice of what's happening around you. Gary is a husband and father with two girls still at home. He and I have different professional and personal backgrounds, yet our journey to joining the bucket list brigade traversed similar paths. Gary has a background in business and computer programming. While I have bounced from TV station to TV station, up and down the radio dial and back again, Gary has had only three jobs in thirty years! And yet as I was writing this chapter, Gary came to mind. It is so important to learn from those around us. The day I contacted Gary to see if he might be interested in contributing to this particular part of the book, he just about dropped the phone. He had been doing a lot of pondering and praying about a fairly recent decision to go out on his own full-time. And it all started, as in my case, with a major reversion to the Catholic Church.

> In 2004, I started experiencing some health issues. Although they turned out to be nothing, at the time I was convinced that I was going to die. This little "scare" proved to be a huge blessing because it gave me the "kick in the pants" that I needed to begin learning about my Catholic Faith. Thinking that I could soon be meeting the Lord was enough to motivate a very lukewarm Catholic into someone

who desired to have a personal relationship with the Lord and be able to share the teachings of the Church with others. After studying and listening to Catholic radio for a few years, I felt a desire to create a website designed to help other lukewarm Catholics learn about the teachings of the Church and be able to get to know Christ as a person. Despite having no Web experience, I stumbled on a "create your own website" ad, and in a few days, "FollowingTheTruth.com" went live.

Writing was never part of Gary's original idea for his website, but he felt compelled to start a blog. And here's where "taking notice" comes in. In addition to responding to your own gut feelings, which in many cases are direction from the Holy Spirit, God will also give you plenty of guidance along the way. As Nick Synko teaches, this guidance can sometimes come in the form of affirmations of a particular gift that you might not have recognized. In Gary's case, a Catholic producer came across one of his articles and was impressed, and all of a sudden Gary was being interviewed on national Catholic radio.

I was thrilled and scared to death at the same time. I fully believed that I'd go on one time and that would be the end of my radio career. Realizing that I was in over my head, I asked the Lord to speak through me and to give me the necessary words. Surprisingly, I was asked to appear on the show again (and again) and I'm now a regular guest.

As Nick Synko explains, and as Gary and I found out, God had already given us exactly what we needed—we just needed to discover it ourselves:

I had been telling clients and students for years that once you are self-aware and know what you have as assets, you will be prepared to analyze and determine what you should do with what you have been gifted and experienced. In other words, God has equipped you for all he wants you to achieve. Said otherwise, the best use of any tool is that for which it is made. By determining how He has equipped a person similarly, we can determine His intended use.

Gary Zimak agrees. The best test, Gary insists, is that old school of hard knocks and trial and error, all the while remembering that God might be up to something:

It started to become obvious that, despite all of my imperfections and extreme shyness (you read that

right, I've always been extremely shy and intro-
verted), God was using me to proclaim His message. Feeling energized and called by the Lord, I
continued to appear on many Catholic radio programs and even started my own show on Internet
radio while still maintaining a full-time day job as a
project manager.

God continued to speak to Gary and to grab his
attention. No, Gary didn't lose his mind and start
hearing voices. But he did get a sense that God was
trying to reach him through other people and through
music:

Now, here's where the story really gets interesting.
In late 2009, I took a vacation day and went with
my wife and kids to Manasquan, New Jersey. It's
a shore town where my wife lived when she was a
child, and we sometimes visit for day trips. While
Eileen and the girls were shopping, I took a break
and sat on a bench listening to my iPod. Although
the majority of the music on my iPod was '50s, '60s,
'70s and '80s pop (my usual music of choice), I had
recently downloaded a few songs by the Catholic
singer John Michael Talbot. As I sat enjoying the
warm sun, I listened to two of his songs back to
back: "Here I Am, Lord" and "Be Not Afraid."
Immediately after this, I got the "crazy" thought

that the Lord may be calling me to work for Him full-time and that I shouldn't be afraid. Being the practical and conservative person that I am, I immediately dismissed the idea, thinking that "normal" people don't do things like this.

But, hey, why be normal? Using the word *normal* in conjunction with the terms *discernments* and *God's will* makes no sense anyway and ends up being a giant oxymoron. There is no definition of *normal* when God has a unique bucket list for each person.

Gary and I can easily identify with those who enroll in Nick Syko's Careers Through Faith seminars. CTF participants have taken stock enough to know that their current work ain't what it used to be. While enjoying his appearances in Catholic media and his efforts in online ministry, Gary's insists that his day job was sucking the life out of him. He really had a strong desire to quit that job, but being the main breadwinner in the family, he was worried about paying the bills. However, these steps are all about working through a process. Even though Gary was getting some pushback, Nick Synko says it's crucial to weigh everything while still not crossing those interests completely off the flip charts:

What may only be a minor interest may well be the seed of greater opportunity and God's calling. Read the Parable of the Talents in Matthew 25:14–30 to understand how important even a minor or one interest or talent may be when given in service to God.

And remember that closed doors or obstacles, as Gary discovered, may really be opportunities. Trying to play it safe didn't work. So he kept doing more radio and more writing. As he continued to develop his website and his ministry, he was also learning more about himself spiritually. At first he couldn't understand why God would not give him full-time work as an evangelist. Then he realized he was still pursuing his own agenda. His "aha" moment came when the decision to leave his day job was actually made for him. He was laid off.

Although my "Following the Truth" apostolate existed for four years, I never earned one cent from my work. Since I had a full-time job, I paid for all of the expenses and never felt the need to raise money. Things would now change in a hurry! Although it didn't immediately feel like it (I'll never forget the walk to my supervisor's office that day . . . we all knew what it meant), Eileen and I viewed the layoff as an answered prayer. When I wondered whether I should begin to look for a new job, Eileen reassured me that I should "go for it" and begin working full-time for the Lord.

Gary is keeping very busy these days writing, speaking, and answering questions about faith on many Catholic radio shows. And talk about turning misery into ministry: Gary's first book was all about dealing with worry, *A Worrier's Guide to the Bible: 50 Verses to Ease Anxieties.*

Taking stock or inventory is, as Gary and I have learned firsthand, just the beginning of the bucket list journey. As Nick Synko insists:

Discovering your inner S.A.I.N.T. will give you clarity and a deeper understanding of who you are today and the potential you possess.

Taking stock is obviously not for sissies. So grab the Gatorade! It requires a lot of energy, time, thought, prayer, and interaction, especially with God. And it pretty much comes with the guarantee that your life is going to be different. Better, yes, eventually, but also different. So if you're not ready to stretch yourself and leave behind the status quo . . . as my cousins on the East Coast would say, "Fuhgeddaboudit!"

7

Live the Good Life

*Everyone has inside of him a piece of good news.
The good news is that you don't know how great
you can be! How much you can love! What you
can accomplish and what your potential is!*
—Anne Frank

Every one of us probably has a "Marie Barone" in the family. You know, the one who puts the plastic on the "good" furniture in the living room and hides the fancy hand towels and dishes for special occasions, but those special occasions never seem to materialize. One of the funniest episodes of the award-winning TV sitcom *Everybody Loves Raymond*, a program that has taken on a life of its own in rerun land, is built around Raymond, his brother Robert, and their crotchety father, Frank, all trying to get Marie, the matriarch of the New York Italian American family, to relax and really live with the good stuff.

Anyone who comes from an ethnic background would be rolling on the floor watching the following scene that the actors portray so realistically. After some very emotional and very loud discussions, Marie insists she can relax just as much as the next person. She gives in and takes the plastic covers off the couch. But it doesn't last long. Raymond and the guys are so paranoid about spilling their soda on the good furniture that they just can't get comfortable. Who could blame them? Marie's idea of "relaxing" includes standing over the men as they tried to settle back into a piece of furniture that for most of their lives had been in the infamous *no tocarre*—"don't touch"—category. So the plastic goes back on, and the good furniture goes unused . . . and unappreciated.

God wants us to say "so long" to Marie Barone and her plastic covers. And "hello" to living in the present, making the most of each moment, and embracing the good life. But what exactly do we mean by the good life? Let me illustrate.

During one of our visits to my husband's hometown in Scranton, Pennsylvania, we passed a lovely interior design store called Live with It. It's a great place to browse and to shop, and doing both has become a habit of ours. At first I found the name rather odd. Then I realized it totally captures their concept of decorating a house or apartment with beautiful artwork, floral arrangements, or figurines. Beauty is meant to be enjoyed and celebrated. The idea is to actually live with that special item and share the beauty with others. You want it on the dining room table, the coffee table, the living room—in a place you pass by or spend time in several times a day. You don't want to be like Marie and keep the Waterford crystal or the Belleek vase in the back of the hall closet. As Psalm 139:14–16 explains, we are a lot more significant than expensive dishware or linens:

> I praise you, because I am wonderfully made. Wonderful are your works! My very self you know. My bones are not hidden from you, when I was being made in secret, fashioned in the depths of the earth. Your eyes saw me unformed; in your book all are written down; my days were shaped, before one came to be.

As I was preparing for an interview with my friend and Christian career counselor Nick Synko, I thought about living in the moment. The segment on my daily radio program would be highlighting one of his Careers Through Faith seminars. I love the concept Nick offers in Careers Through Faith, because it isn't about a quick fix or merely finding a "better job." His sessions got me thinking about the long list of folks I have known over the years who spend most of their working hours in jobs they don't really enjoy.

They're a lot like the Marie Barones of the world: afraid to enjoy or maybe even discover the good stuff about themselves. So instead of living with it, they lock away the desires of their heart along with their natural talents or put them on a bucket list, thinking that someday they'll get around to pursuing what they truly love. Nick Synko explains that those who are serious about happiness need to answer some tough questions:

> My belief is that the most insightful survey question to ask is "If it were no longer economically necessary for you to work, would you remain in your current job?" While national surveys and such statistics are often interesting, the most relevant approach to this question is always individual. "Would you?" And "If not, what are you going to do about it?"

The Conference Board, a global business research association, regularly examines job satisfaction. One of their reports pointed to tough economic times as a big reason Americans aren't very anxious to get to the office. Workers are still having difficulty finding a job that both challenges them and meets their financial needs. The experts claim the cases of on-the-job blues have been rising steadily, thanks at least in part to the struggling economy. Another survey, conducted by CBS News, confirms the Conference Board statistics: fewer than half of those polled, or about 47 percent, believed they were better off than their parents' generation. That figure was down some 15 percent from a similar survey in 2007.

While economic woes can't be ignored, there are several other key reasons why there are an awful lot of unhappy professionals and unfinished masterpieces. Maybe you stay put because your job is what you have always wanted to do and you don't know anything else, but deep inside there is a longing to somehow still use some of your untapped God-given talents. Or maybe you were pressured by your parents to pursue a particular path, and now it seems like you're trapped.

However, Scripture tells us that despite our fears, we are not allowed to sit on the sidelines. In the Parable of the Talents (Matthew 25:14–30; Luke 19:12–28), we see the fate of the servant who was responsible for making the most of one talent, a "talent" here referring to a form of currency. The fear factor—fear of his master, fear of failure, or maybe both—takes over, and he fails. In constrast, two other slaves, one who was given five talents and another who was given two talents, take the master's cash and double the money. The master then calls them good and faithful servants and quickly rewards them for their efforts by giving them more responsibilities and talents. Not so with servant number one:

> Then the one who had received the one talent came forward and said, "Master, I knew you were a demanding person, harvesting where you did not plant and gathering where you did not scatter; so out of fear I went off and buried your talent in the ground. Here it is back."
>
> His master said to him in reply, "You wicked, lazy servant! So you knew that I harvest where I did not plant and gather where I did not scatter? Should you not then have put my money in the bank so that I could have got it back with interest on my return? Now then! Take the talent from him and give it to the one with ten. For to everyone who has, more will be given and he will grow rich; but from the one who has not, even what he has will be taken away. And throw this useless servant into the darkness outside, where there will be wailing and grinding of teeth." (Matthew 25:24–30)

Only God knows what is in a person's heart and what types of challenges a man or woman might be facing. Coming to terms with disappointment and unfulfilled hopes and expectations is a painful process. It's also important to be able to balance those feelings with reality. God doesn't expect a person with a family to up and suddenly quit a job. However, we need to be honest enough with God and ourselves to discern whether we may be using our circumstances as an excuse to maintain the status quo. Our decisions have consequences and impact many more people than just ourselves. That's why, as we see in the Parable of the Talents, we can't take a shortsighted approach. We all have circles of people we touch. It's necessary to step back and take a look at the situation from a much broader perspective. Our actions, both positive and negative, have a ripple effect.

Before I walked away from news reporting, my dissatisfaction level had begun to take its toll. As a reporter, it was my job to disseminate information to the general public about a variety of topics. But I felt as if my work had devolved into covering senseless crimes. I went home every day thinking, *What good am I actually doing?* In some ways, I might have been providing a platform for families and crime victims to express their grief, but the frequency of airing one tragedy after the next began to make me feel I was invading their privacy. Often I wasn't given enough time to allow those I interviewed to gather their thoughts before putting them on camera. I didn't feel the station had their best interests in mind.

It hit me one day while interviewing the relatives of a murder victim that my frustration and cynicism could lead to sloppy or careless reporting. As much as

I had grown to dislike the "if it bleeds, it leads" approach to news, it was still my responsibility to report accurate information. This family, as distraught as they were, had a story to tell and had entrusted that story to me. Whether the stories were good, bad, or ugly, my lousy attitude had the potential to damage a lot more than just my journalistic reputation.

There is plenty of research, some of it dating back more than twenty years, indicating how low job satisfaction can be far-reaching at the company level, whether the company is a small business or a large corporation. A report published in the *International Archives of Occupational and Environmental Health* found that workers reporting low job satisfaction experienced several other negative consequences. Job stress is a big factor when it comes to job satisfaction, and the negativity can lead to an overall decrease in workplace morale. It's true that misery loves company. The study found that when employees see someone who is miserable at work, it begins to color how the other employees view their jobs, and the bad attitude can spread quickly.

My own job stress in my job as a TV news reporter showed, and I had more and more difficulty leaving the job at the office. For a time, I couldn't see any way out of my situation. I didn't know how to do anything but news reporting, or so I thought. What

I needed was a new pair of glasses. I needed to see myself as God saw me: a person with a number of different communications talents that could be used for a glory much greater than my own. In many ways, it was a lot easier for me to say "so long" than for most. My husband had a well-paying job. We had learned, thanks mainly to the insecurity of the broadcasting business, to live well below our means. We did lose a lot of ground at first in terms of our savings, and we made other changes to our lifestyle. While I was busy reinventing myself, staycations replaced those overseas trips, and Saturday nights at our favorite restaurants turned into dinner at home with a much cheaper wine.

Such adjustments are miniscule compared with the responsibilities of someone who is the main provider in the family. It's a lot more difficult to move on to better and more meaningful work when the bills from the pediatrician, the orthodontist, and the car mechanic keep coming in. But it's not impossible. If you're yearning to find more meaningful work to satisfy your soul, start by taking a few small steps. In addition to the S.A.I.N.T. exercise, continue to conduct your own home version of Nick Synko's Careers Through Faith program. You've already outlined your skills, abilities, interests, and talents on paper. Now it's time to add your hopes, dreams, and desires.

Think about some activity that you could do that would not impact the day job but would allow you to move toward the direction of God's bucket list.

Here are a few other suggestions on how to get started:

- Seek outside input. (Start with family and close friends, then seek spiritual and professional advice from trusted sources.)
- Seek volunteer opportunities in your area of interest. (This is a win-win situation, as helping others is always uplifting and can also provide an outlet for your passion.)
- Go on a retreat. (Remember the importance of taking stock? Big decisions require a lot of thought and prayer. Getting away from the routine and getting closer to God will help you focus and prioritize.)
- Think of the word *fear* as nothing more than "false evidence appearing real." (Concentrate on the positive instead of the negative. Things are never as scary as they seem.)

We all need to be more like the servants who were given multiple talents. At first they most likely shared some of the same feelings expressed by the servant with one talent. Their master is described as someone who had a great deal of power and influence, so a little bit of fear would be normal. I get the sense that they were moved by the master's obvious level of trust and expectancy. "Wow," I can just hear them saying. "He must think we are pretty special to leave us with a good part of his property." They were able to put aside their fear. The servant with one talent allowed all kinds of alarming scenarios about his master to develop in his mind. He convinced himself that his fears were reality. So he was frozen in that fear and as a result his talent was just sitting there hidden away, doing nothing. How many times have we also left our gifts and talents sealed tightly in that box in our hearts? I know what it is like to worry about how finally unwrapping those desires and talents might bring about a lot of challenges and changes. But I also knew I did not want to live with any regrets. At least I could say I tried. Another reason to remove that plastic and find that true calling sooner than later.

Have you ever given someone a very special or somewhat extravagant gift only to learn later that it's still in the box in the basement? Your friend or loved one tells you it's just too good and too fragile. It might break, so it's better off remaining safely tucked away. You would be hurt, disappointed, and a bit insulted. That gift was meant for the recipient to enjoy. Marie Barone is a lot like that. She isn't a bad person. She loves her family to a fault, and she has some other endearing qualities, even though her TV daughter-in-law Debra might strongly disagree. Marie, however, does personify a trap a lot of us fall into from time to time. For whatever reason, she thinks that the good stuff is not meant to be part of her daily experience. But read on, and see why you don't have to keep the plastic covers on the couch or the good china packed away any longer.

8.

Live like You're Loved

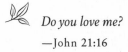 *Do you love me?*
—John 21:16

I have always identified with Saint Peter. As with Saint Peter, there have been times in my relationship with God when I really thought I was doing or saying just the right thing, and then before I could shout out an "Amen," I was falling flat on my face. Peter was also known for saying yes too quickly, then running in the opposite direction when the going got a little bit too tough. Peter denied Christ three times. I wish I could say my denials of Jesus are so few, but that's hardly the case. If the man upon whom the Church was built can make some major mistakes, then there is still hope for me.

I also love Saint Peter because his sadness and re-morse over his denying Christ are signs of his deep love for God. The Gospel of Saint John tells us about the beautiful exchange between Christ and Peter, the exchange that led to what the Catholic Church refers to as the Primacy of Peter, or the institution of the papacy. This special love story happened along the Sea of Galilee after Jesus's resurrection. Peter, lost in his sorrow, didn't know what else to do, so he decided to go fishing. He sees someone standing on the shore. Then he realizes that someone is Jesus! He doesn't wait for the boat to make it to land. He jumps right in the water and starts heading for the beach:

> When Simon Peter heard it was the Lord, he tucked in his garment, for he was lightly clad, and jumped into the sea. (John 21:7)

Peter sprang into the sea because he knew Jesus was giving him another chance at love. The Church of the Primacy of St. Peter, on the north shore of the Sea of Galilee, commemorates this event and is my favorite church in the Holy Land. Though not nearly as complex, dramatic, and mystifying as the Church of the Holy Sepulcher in Jerusalem or the Church of the Nativity in Bethlehem, it's a place of healing and new beginnings. It's a place where I fall in love with Jesus all over again—and when you come right down to it, falling in love with Jesus is all that matters.

Pilgrims tend to focus on the sites of Jesus's birth, death, and resurrection for obvious reasons. The Church of the Primacy is a simple structure built of black basalt. It doesn't contain any stunning religious art inside—just a simple altar near a piece of flat rock believed to be the place where Jesus cooked breakfast for His disciples. What tugs at my heart is the exchange that occurred here two thousand years ago between Jesus and Peter, the first pope. According to John 21:9–17:

> When they climbed out on shore, they saw a charcoal fire with fish on it and bread. Jesus said to them, "Bring some of the fish you just caught." So Simon Peter went over and dragged the net ashore full of one hundred fifty-three large fish. Even though there were so many, the net was not torn. Jesus said to them, "Come, have breakfast." And none of the disciples dared to ask him, "Who are you?" because they realized it was the Lord. Jesus came over and took the bread and gave it to them, and in like manner the fish. This was now the third time Jesus was revealed to his disciples after being raised from the dead.
>
> When they had finished breakfast, Jesus said to Simon Peter, "Simon, son of John, do you love me more than these?" He said to him, "Yes, Lord, you know that I love you." He said to him, "Feed my lambs." He then said to him a second time, "Simon, son of John, do you love me?" He said to him, "Yes, Lord, you know that I love you." He said to him,

"Tend my sheep." He said to him the third time, "Simon, son of John, do you love me?" Peter was distressed that he had said to him a third time, "Do you love me?" and he said to him, "Lord, you know everything; you know that I love you." Jesus said to him, "Feed my sheep."

So there they are, sitting around a charcoal fire. The last time Peter was sitting by a charcoal fire was in Jerusalem the night the cock crowed after he denied knowing Jesus. The scene now taking place days later on the shore wasn't about rubbing salt in the wound. This was about redemption. Peter denied Christ three times, and now Jesus was giving Peter the chance to start all over again.

The idea that real love allows clean slates and fresh starts is presented later in the New Testament in the words of Saint Paul—in that well-known reading from 1 Corinthians that's so popular at weddings. As a matter of fact, I can't remember any wedding my husband and I have attended that didn't include 1 Corinthians 13:1–13.

If I speak in human and angelic tongues but do not have love, I am a resounding gong or a clashing cymbal. And if I have the gift of prophecy and comprehend all mysteries and all knowledge, and if

I have all faith so as to move mountains but do not have love, I am nothing. If I give away everything I own, and if I hand my body over so that I may boast but do not have love, I gain nothing. Love is patient, love is kind. It is not jealous, love is not pompous, it is not inflated, it is not rude, it does not seek its own interests, it is not quick-tempered, it does not brood over injury, it does not rejoice over wrongdoing but rejoices with the truth. It bears all things, believes all things, hopes all things, endures all things. Love never fails. (1 Corinthians 13:1–7)

Jesus was *showing* Peter what true love was all about that morning along the shore. And so is Saint Paul. The reading from 1 Corinthians calls for us to treat others as Christ treated Peter. How many times, I'm ashamed to say, did I roll my eyes as I was sitting in church at yet another wedding Mass hearing those familiar words? Mind you, they were only familiar to me because they were so popular with brides and grooms, not because I had any understanding of Scripture. After I began studying the Bible, I realized just how poignant these verses are, and not just for newlyweds:

If there are prophecies, they will be brought to nothing; if tongues, they will cease; if knowledge, it will be brought to nothing. For we know partially and we prophesy partially, but when the perfect comes, the partial will pass away. (1 Corinthians 13:8–10)

We can jump through all the hoops, attend all the right vocation seminars and Christian conferences, but if we don't really love God above everything else, it's not going to stick, at least not for very long.

Most of us have experienced true love in some form. It may have been through marriage and meeting Mr. or Mrs. Right. Perhaps you've been blessed with children and fell crazy in love the first day your baby was placed in your arms. Both marriage and parenting are a mixed bag. These relationships are meant to be lifelong commitments, and they come complete with good times and bad. But who would pass on the chance for this kind of real, true love?

Falling in love is something we humans are familiar with as a lived experience. It's the dirty dishes, the dirty diapers, the birthday parties, the family vacations. It's the profound realness of being in a relationship, being able to say "I'm sorry" and give and receive forgiveness. We have made these types of efforts and spoken these words with husbands, wives, sons, and daughters, and all for the sake of love. There are no guarantees that the marriage will stay intact or that the kids will remain close. That's the risk we take when we love another human being. There is, however, a guarantee with God:

For He has said, "I will never fail you nor forsake you." Hence we can confidently say "The Lord is my helper, I will not be afraid. (Hebrews 13:5–6)

And surely I am with you always to the very end of the age. (Matthew 28:20)

The Lord appeared to us in the past saying: "I have loved you with an everlasting love. I have drawn you with unfailing kindness." (Jeremiah 31:3)

For I am convinced that neither death nor life, nor angels, nor principalities, nor things present nor things to come, nor powers, nor height, nor depth, nor anything else in all creation, will be able to separate us from the love of God Jesus our Lord." (Romans 8:38–39)

So why aren't we willing to take the risk in loving Jesus? Why do we, at first, give in to despair, as Saint Peter did? Why does this idea of "falling in love" with God, or being in "a relationship" with Him seem so foreign and strange? Maybe we're afraid we'll be expected to stand on a street corner and scream

"Repent, the end is near," or to go live in a monastery somewhere without Internet access and satellite TV? We might think we have to have one of those experiences in which the clouds part and everything is made perfectly clear. Fear not. In my twelve years as a talk show host, I think I have interviewed maybe three or four people who have had what we would call a love-at-first-sight encounter with God. These people have literally been infused with a sudden burst of grace and instantaneously know that God is real. They are filled with an overwhelming love for Him, and everything changes. Based on their witness and the fruit of their ministries, it's obvious these folks are for real. They are also a rarity. So what does that mean for the rest of us? Deep down, I suspect this falling-in-love thing seems so odd and unreal because we don't really know how much God loves us.

Love at first sight may happen on occasion, but a deep love develops over the days, months, and years of being together. When we first meet someone special, we do whatever it takes to get to know them better. When Dominick and I began dating, we spent hours talking on the phone, writing notes, and sending special cards. We quickly became attached at the hip and did everything together. I even found myself attending his softball games and bowling-league outings just to be near him. I intentionally made him a big part of my life. How many of us have done that with God?

When it comes to Catholics, apparently not too many. In her book *Forming Intentional Disciples: The Path to Knowing and Following Jesus*, Sherry Weddell says we should embrace the idea of a similar living experience of Jesus. She draws from the Lineamenta, the guidelines for the 2012 Synod of Bishops, called by Pope Emeritus Benedict XVI to focus on the New Evangelization:

> Genuine Catholic identity flows from the experience of discipleship. As the Lineamenta notes:
>
> "What is not believed or lived cannot be transmitted. . . . The Gospel can only be transmitted on the basis of 'being' with Jesus and living with Jesus the experience of the Father, in the Spirit, and in a corresponding way of 'feeling' compelled to proclaim and share what is lived as a good and something positive and beautiful."

We understand the idea of living and believing from the human perspective when it comes to our families and friends. We know them because we have been with them and experienced them. We need to apply the same type of thought and action to our relationship with God. Weddell writes in *Forming*

Intentional Disciples that we have no idea what this relationship with God is supposed to look like:

> Widespread neglect of the interior journey of discipleship has unintentionally fostered an immense chasm between what the Church teaches is normal and what many Catholics in the pews have learned to regard as normal. Many lifelong Catholics have never seen personal discipleship lived overtly or talked about in an explicit manner in their family or parish. It is difficult to believe in and live something that you have never heard anyone else talk about or seen anyone else live.

The sad truth is that they really haven't seen anyone who has fallen head over heels in love with Jesus. That's what John Paul II was trying to impart in his papal encyclical *Redemptoris Missio* ("Mission of the Redeemer") when he referenced the New Evangelization. You and I probably know people who have estranged family members. We might even have a few of those ourselves. You haven't seen them for years, and they're probably not going to show up at the next graduation party or wedding reception, yet they still haven't disowned you to the point of changing their name. They're just not interested in keeping in touch. John Paul II says in *Redemptoris Missio* that this is what's happened with the Christian faith in many parts of the world:

> [P]articularly in countries with ancient Christian roots and occasionally in the younger Churches as well . . . entire groups of the baptized have lost a sense of the faith, or even no longer consider themselves members of the Church, and live life far removed from Christ and his gospel. In this case what is needed is a "new evangelization" or a "re-evangelization.

Our Protestant brothers and sisters refer to having a "personal relationship" with Christ. In the Catholic Church, we can, if we embrace it, have the most personal relationship with Jesus, as we have the gift of being able to receive Him body, blood, soul, and divinity through the Eucharist. But unless we have fallen in love with Jesus, the sacraments are an unopened gift. As I've mentioned earlier, if Catholics really knew what they had in the Eucharist, why would anyone go anywhere else?

In a 2011 address to the bishops of the Philippines, Pope Emeritus Benedict XVI said the call for a personal relationship with Christ must be preached from the pulpit. He called a personal relationship with Christ the key to evangelization, as well as the key to complete fulfillment:

> Above all, to keep God at the center of the life of the faithful, the preaching of you and your clergy must be personal in its focus so that each Catholic will grasp in his or her innermost depths the life-transforming fact that God exists, that he loves us, and that in Christ he answers the deepest questions of our lives. Your great task in evangelization is therefore to propose a personal relationship with Christ as key to complete fulfillment. In this context, the second Plenary Council of the Philippines continues to have beneficial effects, the result being that many dioceses have formed pastoral programs focused on conveying the good news of salvation. At the same time, it must be recognized that new initiatives in evangelization will only be fruitful if, by the grace of God, those proposing them are people who truly believe and live the message of the Gospel themselves."

There we go again . . . yet one more reference to the lived experience of a relationship with God. The pope is telling the bishops that the only way to cut through all the "stuff" in people's lives is to help them fall in love with God. Benedict continues in his address:

> While the Philippines continue to face many challenges in the area of economic development, we must recognize that these obstacles to a life of happiness and fulfillment are not the only stumbling blocks that must be addressed by the Church. Filipino culture is also confronted with the more subtle questions inherent to the secularism, materialism, and consumerism of our times. When self-sufficiency and freedom are severed from their dependence upon and completion in God, the human person creates for himself a false destiny and loses sight of the eternal joy for which he has been made. The path to rediscovering humanity's true destiny can only be found in the reestablishment of the priority of God in the heart and mind of every person.

Saint Peter reestablished God in his heart and mind by responding to the love and forgiveness being offered by Christ. In his address to the bishops, Pope Emeritus Benedict says we need to do the same:

> In order to confront the questions of our times, the laity need to hear the Gospel message in its fullness, to understand its implications for their personal

lives and for society in general, and thus be constantly converted to the Lord.

So here we are at the end of this thought experiment concerning God's bucket list for our happiness.

- Live with stillness
- Live your passion
- Live with instruction
- Live in the mess
- Live with understanding
- Live by confession
- Live the good life

Now we're taking a close-up look at probably the most important bucket list item for success in life: falling in love with God and putting Him first.

Being in relationship with God is not just about the initial "I do." Saint Peter taught me a lot about that. He was with Jesus in the beginning of His early ministry . . . until the moment the going got very tough. Then he was long gone and in hiding with most of the other apostles. Peter had to learn that Jesus allows U-turns. But that lesson isn't just for the first pope or the other great saints. It's for each of us if we allow ourselves to love Jesus with our whole heart, mind, soul, and strength. And how does He love in return?

I love you with an everlasting love. (Jeremiah 31:3)

I rejoice over you with singing. (Zephaniah 3:17)

I am the Alpha and the Omega, the First, and the Last, the Beginning and the End. (Revelation 22:13)

You are my treasured possession. (Exodus 19:5)

Never will I leave you or forsake you. (Hebrews 13:5)

God is love. (1 John 4:8)

Greater love has no one than this; to lay down his life for a friend. (John 15:3)

"For I know the plans I have for you," says the Lord, "plans to prosper you and not to harm you, to give you hope and a future." (Jeremiah 29:11)

And surely I am with you always until the end of the age. (Matthew 28:20)

This type of unconditional love is unheard of in today's culture, where *commitment* is a scary word. But guess what? There is no talk of prenups or quickie divorces here. God is in this thing for the long haul.

Even death, as it says in Romans 8:38, can't separate us from Him. So what's not to love in return about Jesus? Why not give His bucket list for your happiness a try? It will be the best decision you'll ever make. And I guarantee you'll need to buckle those seat belts because you're in for one heck of an exciting ride!

Unfurl the sails and let God steer us where He will.
—*Saint Bede*

Resources

Most of us would never think of heading out the door for an exciting vacation or journey without preparing well in advance and then packing everything we might need to make our experience fruitful and joyful. We take time to research the accommodations. We shop around for the best airfare. And we don't throw just any old thing in that suitcase.

If we want to find and fulfill God's bucket list for our lives, doesn't it make sense to apply at least a similar amount of effort to our search for true joy and happiness? After all, taking a chance at where we spend eternity is a much bigger risk than choosing a bad hotel. We need to prepare for the long journey home by getting to know God. And in order to make sure we stay on the right path, it's important to stay close to Him and grow in faith. That means packing the best resources that will continue to point us in the right direction.

This list is a helpful summary of a variety of Catholic resources, including daily Scripture devotionals, Bible studies, Church teachings, Catholic media outlets, as well as links to some of the top organizations helping Catholics and other concerned Christians engage the culture. Do you have a question about what the Church really says about an issue? Visit one of the easy to navigate and relatively new Vatican news websites. Are you longing for a deeper understanding of God's word? There is bound to be a daily devotional or a Bible study that works for you. Are you concerned about media influence on you and your family? The latest studies and statistics are just a click away.

Including one or more of these items in your spiritual luggage will help you navigate the pilgrim path to heaven. Happy trails!

Daily Catholic Devotionals (online and in print)

Word Among Us: www.Wau.org

Magnificat: www.Magnificat.net

One Bread, One Body: www.PresentationMinistries
.com

Living Faith: www.LivingFaith.com

United States Conference of Catholic Bishops: www
.Usccb.org/bible/readings

Print-on-Demand Catholic Scripture Studies

Catholic Scripture Study International: www.Css
Program.net

The Great Adventure Catholic Bible Study: www
.BibleStudyforCatholics.com

Catholic Way Bible Study: www.Cwbs.org

Women of Grace Study Programs: www.Womenof
Grace.com

Journey through Scripture: www.SalvationHistory.com

Endow: EndowGroups.org

Church Documents and Teachings

Vatican—The Holy See: www.Vatican.va

Catechism of the Catholic Church: www.Vatican.va/
archive/ccc/index.htm

New Advent: www.NewAdvent.org

Catholic Media

Ave Maria Radio: www.AveMariaRadio.net

EWTN Global Catholic Network: www.Ewtn.com

Catholic TV Network: www.CatholicTV.com

Catholic News Outlets (online and in print)

EWTN News: www.EwtnNews.com

Catholic News Agency: www.CatholicNewsAgency.com

National Catholic Register: www.NCRegister.com

Our Sunday Visitor: www.OSV.com

Vatican Radio: http://en.RadioVaticana.va

Vatican News: www.News.va

Zenit News Agency: www.Zenit.org

Pro-Life Resources

Priests for Life: www.PriestsforLife.org

Silent No More Awareness: www.SilentNoMore
    Awareness.org

Coalition on Abortion/Breast Cancer: www.Abortion
    BreastCancer.com

National Right to Life: www.Nrlc.org

Heartbeat International: www.HeartbeatInternational
    .org

Pro-Life Media Outlets

Live Action: www.LiveAction.org

Life Site News: www.LifeSiteNews.com

Life News: www.LifeNews.com

Media Research Organizations

Parents Television Council: www.Parents.tv.org

Culture and Media Institute: www.Mrc.org/cmi

Media Research Center: www.Mrc.org

Family Research Council: www.Frc.org

Morality in Media: www.MoralityinMedia.org

Pew Research Center for People and the Press: www
    .People-Press.org